SERVICE DES

FROM INSIGHT TO IMPLEMENTATION

Andrew Polaine, Lavrans Løvlie, and Ben Reason

Rosenfeld Media
Brooklyn, New York

Service Design: From Insight to Implementation

By Andrew Polaine, Lavrans Løvlie, and Ben Reason

Rosenfeld Media, LLC

457 Third Street, #4R

Brooklyn, New York

11215 USA

On the Web: www.rosenfeldmedia.com

Please send errors to: errata@rosenfeldmedia.com

Publisher: Louis Rosenfeld

Developmental Editor: JoAnn Simony

Managing Editor: Marta Justak

Interior Layout Tech: Danielle Foster

Cover Design: The Heads of State

Indexer: Nancy Guenther

Proofreader: Ben Tedoff

DEDICATION

To my wife, Karin, and my daughter, Alemtsehay, who have both seen the back of my head during the writing of this book more than they deserve

—Andy Polaine

To my wife, Birgit, and children, Lars and Ella, my grounding and my inspiration

—Lavrans Løvlie

To Kate, Otto, and Liberty. I love you.

—Ben Reason

HOW TO USE THIS BOOK

This book was a team effort by Andy Polaine (interaction and service designer, lecturer, and writer) and Lavrans Løvlie and Ben Reason, co-founders of the service design firm live|work. When we formerly worked as interaction and product designers, we realized that what we were often being asked to design was just one part of a larger, more complex service. No matter how well we did our job, if another link in the chain was broken, the entire thing was broken from the customer's perspective. We believe service design offers a way of thinking about these problems as well as clear tools and methods that can help designers, innovators, entrepreneurs, managers, and administrators do something about it.

To date, there are only a few books on service design as we understand the term. Some are collections of academic papers, and one or two give an over-view of methods. They all have their merits, but we wrote this book because we wanted to capture both the philosophy and thinking of service design *and* connect it with very practical ways of *doing* service design.

This book is based on our experience with developing, doing, selling, and teaching service design over several years. It is also a stake in the ground, because we fully expect the practice to continue to develop and grow as more people take up the practice. Our hope is that readers will take what we have written as a starting point, not dogma, and go out and make the world a less annoying, less resource-hungry place.

Who Should Read This Book?

Service design is an activity carried out by a multidisciplinary group of people that includes Web designers, interaction designers, user experience designers, product designers, business strategists, psychologists, ethnographers, infor-mation architects, graphic designers, and project managers. Anyone from these backgrounds should find something valuable within this book's pages.

For many people involved in interaction, user experience, and human-centered design, the insights-gathering methods described in this book will be familiar, as will some of the experience prototyping methods. The mate-rial about the history of service design, blueprinting, service ecologies and propositions, and measurement may be new to people coming from other design disciplines. That said, we think the way the familiar elements fit into the service design context can also be enlightening.

For design directors, marketing people, change agents, managers, and directors of companies and organizations, the case studies and strategic thinking sections will probably be the most inspiring, but we are at pains to point out that the devil is in the execution. The rest of the book deals with the details, which are as important as the vision. Understanding how service designers gather the material they present to stakeholders and what they intend to do with it afterward is important for those who commission designers. This understanding helps everyone work together more fruitfully and speak the same language.

Lastly, this book provides a good framework, set of tools, and case studies for anyone teaching service design, either as a module of another design program or as a complete program in itself. We believe this book contains a valuable mixture of theory and practice. In fact, we would not separate the two.

What's in This Book?

In **Chapter 1, "Insurance Is a Service, Not a Product,"** we begin with a complete case study of Norway's largest insurance company, Gjensidige, to provide an overview of how service design deals with everything from small details to business strategy. This chapter touches on the entire process and puts the rest of the book into context.

Chapter 2, "The Nature of Service Design," examines the history leading to the development of service design, the shift from product to service economies in developed countries, and the ramifications for both design and business. The change in thinking from designing *things* to designing services is greater than many people think. We also make the case for why services need designing at all, and develop a rough taxonomy of services.

Chapters 3 and 4 are all about people—the heart of services. **Chapter 3, "Understanding People and Relationships,"** makes the case that designers working with services need to understand the relationships among all the *people* involved in the service, as well as recognize what opportunities exist for improvement or innovation. **Chapter 4, "Turning Research into Insight and Action,"** offers a range of very practical tools and methods for capturing insights into people's lives and using them to inform the design.

Chapters 5 and 6 tackle the design of services and the methods most specific to service design. In **Chapter 5, "Describing the Service Ecology,"** we show how defining and mapping out the service ecology and developing service blueprints enable designers to understand and describe how services work. **Chapter 6, "Developing the Service Proposition,"** describes how to use the service blueprint to view the complexity of a service through the eyes of customers or users taking a journey over time and across the multiple channels of the delivery of a service.

Chapter 7, "Prototyping Service Experiences," explains the need to work with people outside the office, studio, or lab to prototype the *experience* of a service. Working with people who have a stake in the service as customers or staff enables designers to improve the design before development costs are incurred.

Prototypes need criteria by which we can measure the success or failure of the design, which is the topic of **Chapter 8, "Measuring Services."** We show how measurement can be introduced by service designers to not only monitor a service's performance for management but to empower delivery agents and teams to understand how to improve their role in the overall quality of the service. This does not have to be a case of choosing between customer experience and profits, but can be a win-win situation for all.

Chapter 9, "The Challenges Facing Service Design," is our vision of where we think service design is heading and where its opportunities might lie. This chapter is more speculative, though we use case studies to highlight some of the trends we are seeing in the field.

What Comes with This Book?

This book's companion website (rosenfeldmedia.com/books/service-design/) contains links to resources related to service design and to this book in particular. You'll find more at the live|work site (www.livework.co.uk) and at Andy's site, Playpen (www.polaine.com/playpen). We've also made available the book's diagrams, screenshots, and other illustrations (when possible) under a Creative Commons license for you to download and include in your own presentations. You can find these on Flickr at www.flickr.com/photos/rosenfeldmedia/sets/.

FREQUENTLY
ASKED QUESTIONS

Is service design just customer experience, user experience, or interaction design?

No. They are close cousins to service design, but they are not the same, although work in both customer experience and user experience forms part of service design's remit. We often use the term "user" instead of "customer" in the book, sometimes interchangeably, but sometimes because there are contexts in which a service user might not be a customer or because a service user might also be a service provider (such as a teacher or a nurse). Some projects lend themselves to different language—customers, partners, clients, patients—depending on the project context. Interaction and user experience design are often understood as design for screen-based interactions, but service design covers a broader range of channels than this. Some projects have a strong digital component, of course, so interaction and user experience design have an important part to play, but so do product design, marketing, graphic design, and business and change management. Chapters 2, 5, 6, and 7 reveal the key differences.

Is service design "design thinking"?

Service design does, ideally, work at the strategic business level, connecting business propositions with the details of how they will be delivered. It also champions the idea of designing *with* people and not just *for* them (see Chapter 3). This may mean the use of terms such as "co-production" or methods that include multiple stakeholders within an organization, such as management and frontline staff. We see service design as distinct from design thinking in that it is also about *doing* design and implementation. It also makes use of designers' abilities to visualize and make abstract ideas tangible.

Why are there so many case studies from live|work?

The most obvious answer to this question is that Ben and Lavrans are co-founders of live|work and thus have access to these projects from their own professional experience. The less obvious reason is that many service design projects are about innovation. The results of these projects filter into the public domain through new services or improvements to existing ones, but many companies want to keep their internal activities confidential. On the one hand, this is a good sign that service design adds real value to businesses (see Chapter 8). On the other hand, finding examples not covered by nondisclosure agreements is difficult. This is also the reason why there are few images of behind-the-scenes, in-process project work in the book.

You do not mention [*insert your favorite method here*]. Why not?

We cover many practical methods in Chapter 4, but due to space considerations we left out several methods that are common to all forms of design, concentrating instead on those specific to service design.

Where are your references and sources?

We have provided footnotes for the key references in the book, where appropriate, but we did not want to turn the book into an academic text. That is not to say our arguments are not robust or rigorously researched. We have hundreds of papers and references in our personal libraries. If there is something we should have credited or that is plain wrong, contact us on the book's website (⚑ www.rosenfeldmedia.com/books/service-design/) and we will try to make amends, either on the site or in future editions. The Service Design Network (www.service-design-network.org) and Jeff Howard's excellent sites—Service Design Books (www.servicedesignbooks.org) and Service Design Research (http://howardesign.com/exp/service/index.php)—are good places to find service design resources.

What is the best way to convince management to spend money on service design?

This is the million-dollar question. In Chapter 8 we discuss strategies for measuring the return on investment in service design and how to think about measurement not just in terms of profits but also by considering other metrics in the triple bottom line of economic, social, and ecological benefits.

Are you saying that service design can do everything?

Service design is both broad and deep and necessarily covers many areas and disciplines, but as we argue in Chapter 9, we are not design superheroes who can do it all. Service design works best when designers collaborate with professionals from the disciplines appropriate to the project in hand.

CONTENTS

FOREWORD

If you have a job and live in a city, you may be sheltered from evidence that profound change is under way. But things you can't see can be all too real. City centers bustle, restaurants are full, and shop windows sparkle, but like ghost images on the television, other realities impinge—eerily empty railway stations, newly built malls that never open, well-dressed people lining up at soup kitchens.

These small signs are the visible evidence of a global system under extreme stress. One cause of that stress is the amount of energy needed to keep it all going. A New Yorker today needs about 300,000 kilocalories a day once all the systems, services, networks, and gadgets of modern life are factored in. The difference in energy needed for survival in the preindustrial era and our own complex lives is *60 times*—and rising.

Another cause of stress is the remorseless drive for growth. When the new Italian prime minister, Mario Monti, gave his acceptance speech to the Italian Senate at the end of 2011, he used the word *growth* 28 times and the words *energy* and *resources* zero times. This supposed technocrat neglected even to mention the biophysical basis of the economy that had been put in his charge. He did not see fit to discuss the fact that cars, planes, and freight; buildings and infrastructure; heating, cooling, and lighting; food and water; hospitals and medicines; and information systems and their attendant gadgets all depend on a continuous flow of cheap and intense energy. And this flow is under a duress that can only intensify.

Could economic growth be decoupled from energy growth and expand to infinity that way? Why not grow a service-intensive economy of high-priced haircuts, storytelling, and yoga lessons? This would be a pleasing solution—Service designers save the world!—were it not for one thing: multiplying money *always* expands an economy's physical impacts on the Earth some-where down the line. Indefinite GDP growth on a fixed energy income is not going to happen.

Rather than wait for a global switch to renewables that is not going to happen either, a multitude of communities are exploring how to meet daily life needs in ways that do not depend on the energy throughputs that we have become accustomed to in the industrial world. For every daily life-support system that is unsustainable now—food, shelter, travel, health-care—alternatives are being innovated. These innovations can all benefit from service design expertise.

In the radically lighter economy whose green shoots are now poking above the ground, we will share all resources, such as energy, matter, time, skill, software, space, or food. We will use social systems to do so, and sometimes we will use networked communications. Local conditions, local trading patterns, local networks, local skills, and local culture will remain a critical success factor—and so will service design.

This book is timely and welcome for all these reasons. It will be invaluable for practicing professionals—but also, one hopes, for clients everywhere. Service design is a collaborative activity; everyone involved can benefit from the skills and insights in the pages that follow.

—John Thackara
Marseilles, France, October 2012
Author, *In the Bubble: Designing in a Complex World*

Insurance Is a Service, Not a Product

Insurance rarely comes to mind as an industry that provides a rewarding customer experience. The only time people find out whether their insurance company is actually any good is when they are at their most distressed and vulnerable. When they find out their insurance is awful, there is nothing they can do about it. They are at the mercy of small print they either did not read or did not understand, and they may end up spending hours on the telephone or filling out more paperwork. There should be insurance against mistreatment by insurance companies.

For many insurance companies and the people working for them, the lofty goal is to be the least awful with the minimum effort possible. The insurance market has ended up in a race to the bottom, competing only on price because customers do not understand their complex policies, hence the proliferation of insurance price-comparison websites.

Part of the problem is that insurance is complicated, involves multiple stakeholders and channels, and is a classic example of a service that is often sold as a product. The mix of complexity, human experience, multiple stakeholders, and delivery channels, combined with customer dissatisfaction with an industry stuck in its ways, makes insurance a perfect candidate for disruptive service design.

In 2009, Norway's largest general insurer, Gjensidige (pronounced *yen-SEE-dig-ah*), decided they had had enough of competing in this toxic marketplace on the same level as their competitors. As a financial group with a 150-year history, Gjensidige had a solid position in the market, but they had a strong drive to improve the quality of service they were offering their customers. CEO Helge Leiro Baastad decided that customer orientation should be a main strategic focus and a key competitive advantage for the firm.

A major challenge was a structural one. Gjensidige was organized as a chain of activities from product development to sales, with expert staff working in silos. This industrial model made it difficult to orient the silos to work together to deliver a unified experience to customers. Because Baastad wanted the change to be driven from the heart of the business, he asked marketing director Hans Hanevold and brand director Kim Wikan Barth to leave their jobs for two years to run a company-wide change program called "Extreme Customer Orientation." Both Hanevold and Barth had long track records with the company, enjoyed the respect of their colleagues, and knew how to engage the organization.

Hanevold and Barth began by identifying change agents in every business unit within the company. The underlying principle was that customer orientation should be grown from the inside out rather than being driven by outside consultants, and that the activities should be funded by the business units themselves. To support these activities, they created a company-wide training program, then set about identifying what ultimately amounted to

183 concrete actions to improve customer experience. For some projects, the business units required specialist expertise to fulfil their ambitions, and service designers were hired to help design a better service experience.

Gjensidige embraced service design as a way to help bridge the gaps across the silos and develop their services in more customer-oriented ways. Service design methods helped them create a complete and shared picture of what really provides value to the customer, as well as processes to join up the experiences.

As a lead-up to their change program, Gjensidige employed service designers to challenge their thinking about what the ideal insurance service would look like. The initial task was very broad—Gjensidige wanted to find out about people's behaviors, motivations, and relationships to insurance. It was important, however, not only to understand the mindset of Gjensidige's customers, but also of staff.

The actuaries—the mathematicians and financial wizards who come up with the complex "products" on which insurance is based—belonged to the Product Group. The name of this department was a clue to the shift that was required in the company's internal culture. What the company is really selling is a service. Customers cannot hold insurance in their hands, and their experience of their insurance policy is made up of the service interactions they have with the company. When customers buy a physical product, they can inspect it for build quality, flaws, or damage. It is much harder to do that with services, especially ones that are essentially a contract based on the chance of a future event, such as insurance. Many people buying insurance do not really know what they are buying, and only find out what is covered at the worst possible moment—when disaster strikes. This is not the time to begin haggling over contract details.

Consumer Insights

The approach taken in the Gjensidige project is an example of classic service design—insights research, workshops, service blueprinting, service proposition development, concept sketches and presentations, experience prototyping, testing, and delivery. A fairly small sample of users was involved in the research, but the research went deep. The design team visited and spoke to three people working in Gjensidige's call centers and offices, as well as six customers, to look at both the delivery side and the recipient side of the service. To people used to working with larger data samples, nine people might not sound like enough, but Gjensidige already had a great deal of quantitative information. This information didn't have the detail of the qualitative research needed for an innovation project, however. Quantitative methods are good for creating knowledge and understanding the field, but they are not very useful for translating knowledge into action and helping organizations do something with it. Qualitative studies are very good at bridging this gap.

Five different areas were researched with the participants: insurance in general, social aspects, choices, contact, and tools for staff. What Gjensidige and the service design team discovered were some important differences between what people say and what they do. Some of the insights that were uncovered are described below. Many are questions and needs, and one can see how this kind of research immediately gets the problem-solving juices flowing.

Trust

Insurance is built on trust. When customers pay their premiums, they trust that they will get value for money—and that the insurance company will still exist when they need it. But trust is very fragile. It takes some time to build up and is quickly broken. All the small glitches in delivery—letters sent to the wrong address, billing errors, problems with communication, customers having to repeat details multiple times—damage people's trust in an insurance company. They wonder whether similar chaos happens behind the scenes. Fixing the small glitches can have a big impact on the level of trust.

Comparison and Purchasing Criteria

People say they make insurance purchasing decisions based on quality, but they find it hard to do this in reality. It is very difficult to compare what is inside different insurance policies and make a rational choice. People feel that insurance is not very transparent, especially with regards to quality, so it is easier to compare on price, because money is a fixed variable. This means designers cannot simply trust what customers say they want, but have to work smartly around price and quality issues.

Of course there is room for quality in the market, but with online price-comparison engines, the quality aspect of insurance has completely dropped out of the conversation with customers and all that is left is price. For customers, quality means, "Am I covered? Do I get a rental car when my car is being repaired? Am I actually covered for the things I think should be covered?"

With most other services and products, customers can easily see the differences between the premium version and something cheaper, but not with insurance. Customers are really asking what quality *means*—that is, the difference between the premium and budget products. This raises many other questions, such as what is actually covered and when, how much are the out-of-pocket expenses, and so on. It soon becomes complicated.

As with much service design, the challenge is to make the invisible visible, or to make the *right things* visible and get rid of the noise in the rest of the offering. In the Gjensidige project, then, one of the key challenges was to develop a service proposition that eliminated price as the key deciding factor.

Expectations

People expect an insurance payout when something happens, and they expect help. This is another issue related to quality. Customers who buy a cheap insurance product get money but will not get much help, whereas Gjensidige has a very good system for taking care of people when something happens. For example, when customers have damage to a car, they just take it in for evaluation and Gjensidige issues a rental car and takes care of everything else. This fact needed to be made visible as part of the service proposition.

Employment and Public Benefits

Gjensidige believe they provide all the insurance people might need, but in Norway many people are also covered by some kind of insurance from their employer or union. It is very difficult for people to tell whether they are covered because there is no way for them to see all of this information in one view, all in one place. The challenge is to achieve this in a transparent and trustworthy way for customers.

Social and Cultural Interactions

Many invisible social touchpoints affect the entire service experience. The police, for example, might give insurance advice by saying, "Oh, your cell phone was stolen? Don't even bother contacting your insurance company." Customers who contact Gjensidige do in fact receive a new phone, but people tend to trust that the police are knowledgeable about such issues.

The researchers discovered that many different people were giving advice about insurance who should not be. For example, friends and family were frequently believed to be the best source of insurance advice. People trust their father to give them good advice about an insurance policy more than they trust an insurance agent. (By "agent" here, we mean a representative of Gjensidige because there is very little in the way of an insurance brokerage market in Norway.)

The challenge, then, is how to work together with all of these invisible touchpoints. Insurance originally dates back to a time when people in a small community would pool their money to pay for an accident, such as someone's barn burning down. This stimulated thinking about bringing back this social aspect, because insurance had evolved from a collective effort into these machines that customers don't trust.

Choice

From an insurance specialist point of view, the more options you have the better you will be covered. Covering certain items, such as a new bike, but not others, such as an old PC, allows people to have insurance tailored to their needs.

At the same time, customers want simplicity. The paradox discovered in the insights research was that customers want very simple products, but they want to *feel* like they are making a choice from an array of complex products. The underlying need here is that they do not want to have to choose from lots of options, but they want the *experience* of having made their own choice.

Documents

When it comes to reading insurance papers, one of the typical quotes from interviewees was, "I just can't do it." This connects back to the issue of trust. On the one hand, customers do not read the details of their insurance policies, which means they blindly trust the insurance company to be right. On the other hand, customers do not trust the insurance company because they do not know the details of their policies.

Insurance companies produce enormously long documents, which is the main reason customers do not read them. Customers were saying, "Can't we have just one document and could it be on one page?" but what people actually wanted and needed was a "What if?" structure they could study— one to explain that if *this* happens, the customer will get *that* from the insurance company.

Customers also had no idea where they kept their insurance papers. They know the papers are important and some people *said* they had them securely filed away, but when researchers asked to see them, the papers were in a complete mess. Interviewees would say, "Yes, they're just over here," but it would turn out to be a policy from two years ago and the latest one was still in a pile of papers somewhere. This means that customers have no clue about what they are insured for or what they are even paying.

Another reason people did not know what was in their documents is that most of the text is written by lawyers in "legalese." Over the years, more and more text had been added to these documents without much serious thought about what was still needed. To counter this, Gjensidige reduced the size of their insurance policy documents by 50% to 60% just by taking out extraneous words and simplifying the language as much as legally possible. It took a team of four people a year and a half to do this, but they have done a brilliant job. Gjensidige also gained a small side benefit from reduced printing costs, but the big benefit has been in customer experience.

Company Insights
Filling In the Gaps in Public Benefits

In Norway, people assume that if something bad happens to them, they will be covered by the state, but they have no clue about what actually would be covered and what they should cover themselves. Customers need this information and they need people to talk to who can give them good advice, not just salespeople who are more interested in selling an insurance product than in what customers need.

As in many organizations, the underlying issue is hard targets for sales quotas and organizational structures that actually discourage customer service representatives from taking proper care of people. Gjensidige needed to change the way they measure performance internally so that the benefit could be experienced externally, which meant an internal culture change. Since this change was implemented, everyone's primary measure is customer satisfaction on an individual basis. Customer-facing staff at Gjensidige get daily reports on their own customer satisfaction scores. The main data is gathered by sending customers an e-mail asking if they want to rate their experience after every customer contact by telephone or at a branch office. This feedback is added to a mix of other metrics to make up a comprehensive customer experience measurement system.

Being Personal

When it comes to customer relations, people see straight through things that are meant to be personal but actually are not. Humans are so well attuned to interpersonal interactions that communications such as "personalized" form letters can come across as almost creepy. Worse still, these kinds of faux personal communications are prone to simple glitches, such as old data or typos, leading to personalized life insurance letters being sent to dead relatives, or Mr. Jones being addressed as "Dear Mrs. Jones." There is only one type of personal, and it is to be genuinely personal. For that to happen, of course, the company culture must be one that encourages it and one in which employees feel happy working. Grumpy, stressed people have grumpy, stressed interactions.

Consistent Communication Channels

Respondents wanted Gjensidige to stay on their channel, meaning that if they telephoned, they wanted the company to call them back, not send an e-mail or a letter. If they sent an e-mail, they wanted an e-mail back. Gjensidige made the strategic decision to keep all of their channels open, which is more costly because it is more complicated to manage, but the company believes it is worth the expense because it creates a better customer experience.

Language

Laypeople (customers) really do not understand the language of insurance. A lot of people thought a "premium" was actually a prize, for example. As such, Gjensidige needed to be careful that the insurance language that is clear to them actually means the same thing to their customers across all communication channels.

Formalizing Personal Routines

When researchers visited Gjensidige's offices to interview staff, they saw a lot of sticky notes on salespeople's desks and on their computers (Figure 1.1). Many people had created their own routines for more efficiently dealing with customers. The insight here was that some of the processes developed "on the shop floor" could be adopted and integrated into Gjensidige's systems as standard approaches.

FIGURE 1.1
Sales staff build their own routines to make their process more efficient.

Redesigned processes deeply founded on insight from customers and staff were initially implemented as paper-based routines to avoid waiting for enterprise software to be developed (Figure 1.2). Later, these new routines were built into Gjensidige's new customer relations management (CRM) system (Figure 1.3).

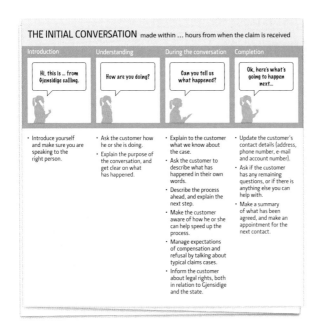

FIGURE 1.2
Paper-based routines were a quick fix for sales staff.

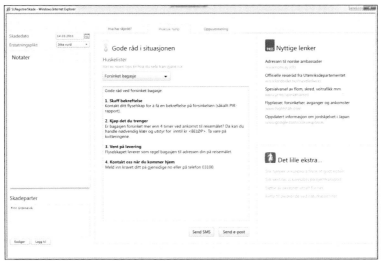

FIGURE 1.3
The new routines were added to the CRM system. A field for customer-specific notes (on the left) functions like a sticky note.

Simplifying IT Infrastructure

All of a customer's details are entered into Gjensidige's S2000 mainframe system, which crunches through the numbers and risk analysis in the actuarial tables to produce an insurance offer. Management said that it was the most brilliant system in the insurance industry in Norway. S2000 is very flexible, which means salespeople can manipulate more parameters than Gjensidige's competitors, but salespeople did not see an advantage in this flexibility. It was too hidden, and in their conversations with customers, the salespeople realized they did not need this flexibility.

Such a flexible system also has the overhead of being more complicated. For instance, a customer could not have a house and a car bundled up in one insurance product. This made it more difficult to create a joined-up experience for the customer.

Putting Insights into Practice

One of the things that hampers product innovation in insurance is the time delay. Organizations only find out whether an innovation will make or lose them money after they see the level of claims, which can take several years. Thus, the insurance industry traditionally is conservative about innovation. The customer insights gathered by the design team helped inspire confidence in bringing new ideas to market.

Using the material from the insights research, Gjensidige ran co-design workshops with different groups within the company and generated 97 ideas, five of which were chosen for further development. Finally, the team came up with one new service proposition.

Gjensidige had about a dozen products for everything to do with people, from individuals to families. From an insurance point of view, this meant that they had a fantastic array of tailor-made products for different eventualities. From a customer point of view, this meant that people felt like they were faced with impossible life insurance choices, such as gambling whether they would die of cancer or in a car accident, because nobody could afford to buy all of the policies and be 100% covered. Customers faced the same dilemma when choosing which possessions to insure—the dog or the laptop?

The breakthrough concept for Gjensidige was to go from offering 50 products to just two: one to cover the individual and his or her family, and one to cover everything they own. From an insurance point of view, this was very radical, but in an example of the value of the expertise that exists inside organizations, the basic idea came from Gunnar Kvan, a very experienced Gjensidige actuary, during a series of design workshops. He suggested that it was possible to think about the company's offerings in a dramatically different way. He had been working on this idea for five years, but had not been able to get people to see his point. He had no way of expressing his view in terms of what it would mean as an experience for customers, but he knew the financial algorithms could be modeled differently. The design team sat down with him and went through how such a service could be put together. It would require hard-core mathematical engineering in a huge spreadsheet running in the background to make it happen.

Experience Prototyping the Service

Anders Kjeseth Valdersnes, the design team's Microsoft Excel maestro, built a prototype of the product in Excel, which had all the tools required to handle the actuarial tables and live information visualization. Rather than spending a week or two designing and coding a Web prototype with a func-tioning back-end database, Anders did it in two days and designed it to look like a website so that it could be tested with customers (Figure 1.4).

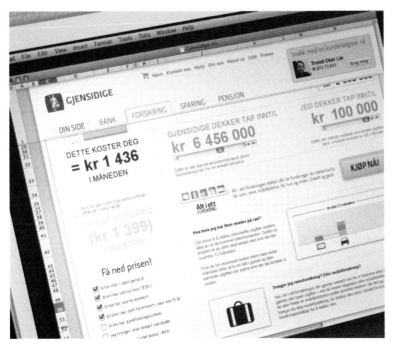

FIGURE 1.4
An experience prototype of the insurance website built in Excel so that the real data could be used when testing with customers.

With this prototype, Gjensidige were able to carry out experience prototype testing with customers discussing and buying insurance, a salesperson selling insurance, and someone trying to make a claim. They tested what it was like for customers to try to buy the services face to face and what it was like for the sales staff. They also tested this process over the phone and observed the process from both sides of the call. To test the claims process, they went through the material with someone who had just had an accident. Actual staff and actual customers took part, and even though they knew they were taking part in testing, the conversations they had were very real. Through this process, the project team learned a lot about what needed to be done to shape, explain, and sell the new service proposition.

It was clear from the prototyping that the new approach changed the conversation from being about buying products to one about service. It meant that customers considered what they could afford on a monthly basis, taking into account what they earned, what was in their "rainy day" savings account, and what they would need in the event of a tragedy. They were able to see the difference their decisions about excess and payout levels made to their premiums, and the conversation was much more open, with the customers in control.

A series of touchpoints were prototyped—the one-page contract, informational leaflets, fake advertisements in a financial newspaper and a tabloid newspaper (Figure 1.5), and the bill customers would receive at the end—so that a broad range of the service experience could be tested.

FIGURE 1.5
Creating fake newspaper ads—one for a financial broadsheet, the other for a tabloid—helped the team understand how the marketing of the service would feel in different contexts.

The one-page contract prototype was a good example of the difference between what people say and what they do (Figure 1.6). Many interviewees said that they did not read long contracts and thus did not know what was in them, leading to a lack of trust in the insurance company. They suggested that a one-page contract would be much friendlier. During prototyping, however, it turned out that customers did not trust a one-page contract either, fearing that too much important detail was hidden from them, as their previous policies had been about 40 pages. Gjensidige ended up creating contracts with around 5 to 10 pages.

Prototypes were also made of the claim process confirmation documents. Traditionally, customers simply received a letter stating, "We have received your claim," which left them uncertain about how the claims process was handled within the company. The redesigned confirmation shows the customer how the process unfolds over time and helps to manage their expectations (Figure 1.7). This way they know when to be patient and let the process take its course, and when they have cause to follow up.

FIGURE 1.6
A prototype of the one-page contract so many interviewees claimed they would prefer. Evidence showed that they did not trust it.

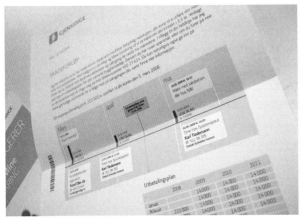

FIGURE 1.7
A prototype of a redesigned claim confirmation. This document manages customer expectations by illustrating how the process unfolds over time.

Lastly, the team prototyped an offer sent out in the mail after a sales call or meeting (Figure 1.8). The insights research showed that this was one of the most crucial touchpoint failures, and the company did not realize the potential of improving it. Previously, customers had an interaction with a salesperson in which they talked through a complicated policy, then would go home and explain it to their partners, but could not remember the details well enough to explain it. Because they could no longer understand it, customers could not make a decision. Redesigning this touchpoint helped people make a decision at home, and the company avoided losing customers because of this hidden problem. This is a good example of how services are created and experienced by interactions between people, often in a completely different context than the usual customer-provider paradigm.

FIGURE 1.8
A prototype of the mailed offer, which is an important touchpoint for customers. This document serves as the focal point for discussion and making a decision. This prototype shows an offer that could be revised by customers before the contract is signed.

The End Is Just the Beginning

The value of gaining real insights from all stakeholders—customers, staff, and management—is only half of the story. Translating these insights into a clear service proposition, and experience prototyping the key touchpoints, are essential. This process allowed for feedback not only on the design of the physical touchpoints themselves but also on the entire service proposition and experience. For the designers and for Gjensidige, it was important to know how something so radical would be perceived in the marketplace. The proto-types were created to test unknowns—for example, Was this a low-end or a high-end offering? The two types of newspaper advertisements helped reveal how the marketing of the service would feel in those different contexts.

Services are usually complex and expensive to roll out. In this case, such a radical change to Gjensidige's offering was not just radical for them, but for the whole industry. It was also clear that it would take a lot of explaining to introduce the concept to their existing, loyal customers. In fact, having only two types of insurance turned out to be too radical even for Gjensidige and the way the entire industry works. This ending might have taken the wind out of the sails of this story, but there is an important innovation lesson to take away from it.

Thinking through radical ideas and prototyping the experience of them helped mature the cultural mindset within the company, and many of the insights have fed into Gjensidige becoming a totally service-oriented company. The Extreme Customer Orientation team acted as champion for the customer experience and the internal changes that needed to happen to deliver it well. A company-wide framework for customer orientation called the "Gjensidige Experience" was implemented. Management understands that this will be a key competitive advantage in the future, building on their vision that "we shall know the customer the best and care the most."

Gjensidige made extraordinary efforts to simplify their insurance poli-cies. They have worked hard to explain the claims process better and have developed a Web-based claims-mapping tool. Pricing has been worked out differently and is now fed into their online calculators. Although the big idea was not used as a whole, many of the small elements have now fed into the company in very concrete ways. Having the big idea helps bundle together lots of smaller, disparate innovations that would not otherwise have seen the light of day. It also helps challenge organizational traditions that may be holding back innovation.

Finally, mapping out the big idea in detail gives organizations an overview of problems and opportunities all in one place, which helps them make stra-tegic decisions about what to deal with when, how those decisions relate to other parts of their business, and how to scale their service innovation up or down according to budgets and resources.

Gjensidige's 183 activities is a very large number of improvements. Some were small; others were large undertakings rolled out over several years. The bottom line is important, of course, but it is not the sole focus. The change process required top-level leadership in all aspects of the busi-ness, from committing to quality in their computer systems by removing glitches, to simplifying their products and language, focusing on the service experience as well as internal funding, and paying attention to branding, education, and measurement.

For example, 130 Gjensidige managers, including the CEO, gathered their own insights by calling 1,000 customers (Figure 1.9). They loved it, because they realized they had not spoken to customers in years and it was often these interactions that had sparked their interest in the business in the first place. Managers were deeply familiar with their statistics about customer satisfaction, as well as the challenges that needed to be addressed. But it made a real difference to experience for themselves how many customers said they really liked Gjensidige, and to feel people's emotions firsthand when they talked about things that didn't work out as they should have. The symbolism of this is important. When a CEO sits down to talk to customers to find out what they think, it sends an important signal to the rest of the organization and the industry.

FIGURE 1.9
Gjensidige CEO Helge Leiro Baastad and 130 of his managers spend a day calling 1,000 random customers to hear what they really think about the company. (Courtesy of Gjensidige)

The results of these kinds of company-wide changes take time to surface. Two and a half years after starting this process, Gjensidige have seen a dramatic rise in their position on the Norwegian National Customer Satisfaction Barometer and have won the two biggest customer satisfaction awards. They have consistently beaten market expectations with their financial results and can prove that they provide their services more efficiently than their peers in Europe and the United States. Still, according to Baastad, the business case for customer orientation should not be seen in isolation. It is a natural part of the bigger story of developing a modern and efficient insurance company that brings real value to employees, shareholders, and customers.

The Nature of Service Design

Like most modern design disciplines, service design can be traced back to the tradition of industrial design, a field defined during the 1920s by a close-knit community of American designers that included Raymond Loewy, Walter Dorwin Teague, Norman Bel Geddes, and Henry Dreyfuss. In Europe, The Bauhaus was central to the birth of industrial design.

What all of these designers had in common was a drive to use new industrial technology to improve people's standard of living. During and after World War I, people were horrified to see the devastation caused by the industrialization of warfare. There was also a great need to restore and improve the material standard of living in Europe and the United States.

On an ideological level, the first generation of industrial designers strove to turn industrialization into a force for good. They focused their talents on figuring out how to use industrial technology to satisfy the fundamental human needs of the day. They explored how industry could create products in more efficient ways, what would make them more useful for people, and how products could contribute to optimism about the future. They created well-designed furniture that was inexpensive enough for the middle class to buy to modernize their homes, and white goods that enabled women to escape some of the drudgery of housework, freeing them to take jobs outside of the home. Cars and trains enabled people to expand their range of travel for work and pleasure.

In the 20th century, the design profession made a huge contribution to the improvement of the standard of living in the developed world. Today, however, this standard of living has reached its natural plateau. We are saturated with material wealth, and our consumption of products is threatening our very existence rather than being a resource for good living.

On the ideological level, our fundamental human needs have also changed. The great challenges facing developed societies today are about sustaining good health, reducing energy and resource consumption, and developing leaner transportation solutions and more resilient financial systems.

The 1920s generation of industrial designers strove to humanize the technology of their day and meet the fundamental material needs of their generation. Service design grows out of a digitally native generation professionally bred on network thinking. Our focus has moved from efficient production to lean consumption, and the value set has moved from standard of living to quality of life.

Why Do Services Need Designing?

As designers, when we build services based on genuine insight into the people who will use them, we can be confident that we will deliver real value. When we make smart use of networks of technology and people, we can simplify complex services and make them more powerful for the customer.

When we build resilience into the design, services will adapt better to change and perform longer for the user. When we apply design consistency to all elements of a service, the human experience will be fulfilling and satisfying. When we measure service performance in the right way, we can prove that service design results in more effective employment of resources—human, capital, and natural.

It would appear easy to study how people experience a service, determine which parts of the delivery are not joined up, and make them all perform well together. In reality, some of the best organizations in the world struggle mightily to design good service experiences.

To explain why companies find it so difficult to design services well, we need to study the nature of services and the way they are delivered.

How Services Differ from Products

The challenge we found when we moved our attention from designing products to designing services was that services are entirely different animals than products. Applying the same mindset to designing a service as to the design of a product can lead to customer-hostile rather than user-friendly results.

Products are discrete objects and, because of this, the companies that make, market, and sell products tend to be separated into departments that specialize in one function and have a vertical chain of command—they operate in *silos* (Figure 2.1).

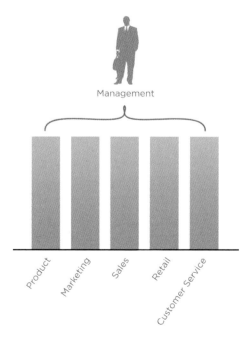

Management

FIGURE 2.1
Where is the customer in this picture? Staff working in silos tend to focus on the efficiency of their step in the value chain rather than the quality of the complete customer experience.

Product   Marketing   Sales   Retail   Customer Service

Two days after setting up our service design consultancy, we received a call from executives at mobile operator Orange with an offer for the kind of project we had dreamed about for several years in our earlier jobs in Web consultancies. Could we help them make the service experience a strategic factor in their development of new services?

At that time, Orange had achieved huge success in the UK market through a strong focus on making mobile telephony clear, simple, and desirable for their customers. Still, they recognized that they lacked tools and processes to make the customer experience drive new service development. Their branding wasn't connected to the services they launched. The website was a marketing channel that didn't help existing customers get more value out of their accounts. Innovation was technology driven rather than customer oriented.

In fact, Orange were organized like a product factory out of the last century, not a modern, market-defining service provider. The company's experts were lodged in silos, and the only people who could see the whole picture of their offering were their customers.

To face this challenge, Orange needed to introduce a design approach that bridged silos and channels. They also needed to introduce the service experience earlier in their strategic thinking so that a vision for the service experience could impact technical and business decisions rather than the other way around. One of the problems with thinking about service experiences at the business level is that it is difficult for people to imagine what something as intangible as a new mobile phone plan would look and feel like. Spreadsheets are a poor medium for conveying human experiences.

To tackle this problem, we created a project called "Tangible Evidence from the Future" and designed the experience of 12 new service propositions ranging from new ways to organize call centers to self-service, online plans. Several of the concepts went to market, including a proposal to change Orange stores from vendors of other brands' phones to places where people could get help with using their mobile services. Another proposition that went to market as "Orange Premier" was a high-end mobile phone plan for people who wanted a unique experience and exceptional service (Figure 2.2).

Orange Premier was a success in the market and introduced a way for Orange to use design as the starting point for business development. We have worked with Orange for the past 10 years to improve their service experience across the board, in projects ranging from innovation strategy to fixing problems with call center delivery.

Our first project with Orange confirmed our thinking that the use of design in this context needed to be reframed from an activity focused on the delivery of products, paper, and interfaces to a process that enables all aspects of a service to play together in a unified experience. We realized that a new landscape was about to open up and that we had to examine how the preconditions for design were changing.

FIGURE 2.2
When we showed Orange how customers could experience a "luxury" account, they decided to launch a proposition with unparalleled attention to the quality of design and customer service.

When companies that sell services are structured in silos, however, problems often arise that affect customer experience. Customers are promised a new mobile phone plan through a website only to find that the assistant in the store knows nothing about it or is not allowed to sell it for the online price. Patients in hospitals are kept in the dark about why they have been waiting for hours, or receive contradictory information during one of the most emotionally difficult times of their lives. *The division of the silos makes sense to the business units, but makes no sense to the customer, who sees the entire offering as one experience.* This problem is something we will return to frequently throughout the book as we look at how to turn this around, quite literally.

Many service companies think they are selling products. The finance sector is a classic example of this mindset, but insurance policies and bank accounts are services with multiple touchpoints of interaction, not products. When something goes wrong, policy holders want the financial compensation, of course, but the difference in value is whether they have an understanding person on the other end of the phone seamlessly guiding them through the claims process versus being sent an unintelligible 20-page form and then having to wait weeks for their money. Many organizations are starting to examine their customer service offering and the value it can bring. This provides great opportunities for service designers.

Services Created in Silos Are Experienced in Bits

The challenge for many service providers is that they are organized in ways that actually prevent them from delivering good service experiences. Often, each bit of the service is well designed, but the service itself hasn't been designed. The problem is that customers don't just care about individual touchpoints. They experience services in totality and base their judgment on how well everything works together to provide them with value (Figure 2.3).

Another complicating factor is that quality can vary dramatically from one service touchpoint to another. If the people who develop online banking don't harmonize quality and coordinate routines with the people who manage the bank's call center, customers are bound to experience disappointment.

The industrial legacy of treating services like products means that services often underperform and disappoint because they cannot be fixed in the same way as problems with products. Services are about interactions between people, and their motivations and behaviors. Marketers and designers often talk of products having personalities, but an iPhone or a Volkswagen doesn't wake up with a hangover, worry about paying the rent, or care who is using them. People do, which is why understanding people is at the heart of service design.

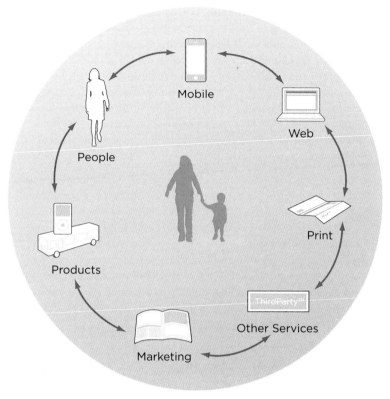

FIGURE 2.3
The service experience is made up of the customer's interactions with many touchpoints, and service quality can be defined by how well the touchpoints work together for the customer.

Services Are Co-produced by People

A fundamental characteristic of services is that they create value only when we use them. A bus service can't get people from point A to point B unless they know where to get on and off. Online banking only provides value when customers virtually enter the bank's machine room through an online banking interface and conduct their own transactions. An empty seat on the train has no value once it has left the station. Even at the dentist's office, nothing will happen unless the patient opens her mouth and tells the dentist where it hurts.

Product-oriented organizations often fail to see the potential of using their customers to make a service more effective. If customers are well informed about bus routes and schedules, they are more likely to get more efficiently from A to B and more inclined to use the bus, reducing their carbon footprint and easing congested roads. If an online bank is well designed, customers don't need to spend time and money in a bank building. Services are co-produced between the provider and users. (We should note that this is not the same as *co-design*, which has customers or users take part in the design process before or after the launch of a product or service.)

On one end of the service spectrum we see network services, such as Facebook, Twitter, and YouTube, that would be useless if people didn't commit millions of hours to produce the content and activity that give these social networks their value. On the other end of the scale, services such as healthcare are most sustainable if fewer people use them. The best way to ensure that hospitals are efficient is for people to "co-produce" their health by keeping themselves in good shape and so they don't need treatment. The biggest missed opportunity in development is that organizations don't think about their customers as valuable, productive assets in the delivery of a service, but as anonymous consumers of products.

A New Technological Landscape: The Network

It is no coincidence that service design has been born as a field of design practice during the last decade. Twenty years ago, the design of services tended to be about hotels and hamburgers. Today, digital platforms are critical to running a business, large or small. The digital landscape of the information age has created radical enablers for new types of service delivery.

Modern service delivery is entirely dependent on digital platforms. Hospitals and banks can't run without immediate electronic access to detailed records, airlines can't sell cheap tickets without algorithms that constantly balance supply and demand, and most people can't do much without the Internet or cell phones. Twenty years ago, cell phones were futuristic gadgets reserved for Wall Street traders and generals; today many people can't even imagine meeting up in a city without a cell phone.

The combination of enterprise systems that store and link vast amounts of data with mass-consumer access to data through the Web and mobile telephony is transforming the way people live their daily lives. At the same time, the quality of service often suffers due to the complexity of linking these systems together in a way that makes sense to customers. This combination of opportunities and problems is the reason why service design has emerged as a specific design approach.

One example of a service that builds on the active participation of its customers to make the service work better is the car-sharing club, which can be found in cities around the world. Car-sharing pioneer Streetcar launched in 2004, but the customer experience needed to be radically improved if Streetcar was to realize its full potential. To persuade people to switch to this new way of using a car, the customer experience had to be better than buying and owning a car. We suggested to Streetcar that the service experience should feel as satisfying as the click of a Volkswagen door—a consistent, solid, and pleasant experience that gives assurance the whole thing is carefully designed (Figure 2.4). This idea may sound trivial, but it is something that the Volkswagen product designers and engineers understand and spend a significant amount of time, money, and effort on.

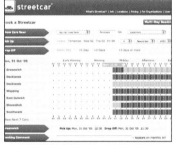

FIGURE 2.4

Streetcar's multiple touchpoints were designed as a holistic, satisfying experience.

sidebar continues on next page

We set about creating a customer experience that would enable Streetcar to over-come their key barriers to growth—lack of comprehension, access, and usability. These were systematically resolved by analyzing the customer journey from first awareness of the brand to regular usage (Figure 2.5).

We were able to identify where customers dropped out of the sign-up process or needed expensive customer support. The service is now clearly communicated as a four-step process: (1) book, (2) unlock, (3) enter PIN, and (4) drive (Figure 2.6). Customers find joining easy with a quick call to Streetcar and the Driver and Vehicle Licensing Agency, and the online booking engine was rebuilt to make it simple to use.

In essence, Streetcar builds on collaboration among the provider, the city, and the customer to make it work. Streetcar provides technology that enables people to rent cars for as little as half an hour. The City of London provides convenient park-ing spots to make the cars more accessible. Customers refuel the cars, keep them clean, and park them where other customers can find them.

Many organizations struggle to utilize the excellent resource that their customers provide. Most customers have a keen interest in getting as much as possible out of the services they use, and by enabling users to step in and co-produce, providers can create win-win solutions.

FIGURE 2.5
Analyzing the customer journey enabled Streetcar to see where customers dropped out of the sign-up process or found the service frustrating.

FIGURE 2.6

The Streetcar service redesign was communicated as a simple four-step process to ensure that new customers immediately understood the service proposition and how it works.

The Service Economy

In developed nations, around 75% of the economy is in the service sector, and this is where most new jobs are created. In Germany, known for its export prowess, the industrial industries dropped 140,000 jobs in 2010 while the service sector added 330,000 jobs, and private nursing services generate more revenue than the entire German automobile industry.[1] To an increasing degree, we also see that the design of services is becoming a key competitive advantage. Physical elements and technology can easily be copied, but service experiences are rooted in company culture and are much harder to replicate. People choose to use the services that they feel give them the best experience for their money, whether they fly low-cost airlines or spend their money on a first-class experience.

Just as industrial design fueled the introduction of new products to the masses in the industrial economy, good service design is key to the successful introduction of new technologies. Design of new models each year became the recipe for maintaining the success of established products. In the service economy, services can be redesigned on a continuing basis to keep a competitive edge in the market.

Some of the greatest opportunities are found where a business model can be changed from a product model to a service model. A case in point is car sharing, where the business model has changed from selling the car as a product to offering access to the service of mobility.

Core Service Values

One way to understand services better—and what makes them different from products—is to examine what it is that people get from services.

There are many breakdowns of the characteristics of services, some of which we will look at later in the measurement chapter. We have been developing a simple way to understand the generic types of value that services deliver to customers by cataloguing every service we have become aware of and then grouping them in relation to three core values: care, access, and response (Figure 2.7). Most services provide customers with at least one of these or, often, a mix of all three.

---

[1] Olaf Gersemann, "Die neue deutsche Arroganz," *Welt am Sonntag*, January 9, 2011, www.welt.de/print/wams/wirtschaft/article12055689/Die-neue-deutsche-Arroganz.html.

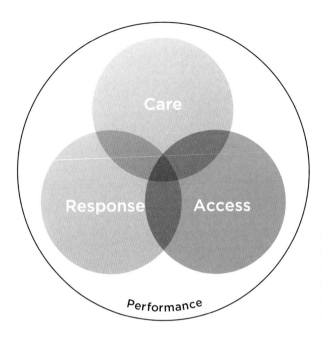

FIGURE 2.7
Core service offerings can be grouped into three primary spheres: care, response, and access.

Services That Care for People or Things

Healthcare is the most obvious case of a service focused on care, but many maintenance services also have care as the core value. A famous example of a care service is the Rolls Royce aviation engine service that monitors aircraft engines in flight and has spare parts ready to be fitted as needed when a plane lands, anywhere in the world.[2]

Care for an object—a car, an air-conditioning system, a wool coat—is provided by auto mechanics, HVAC technicians, or dry cleaners. Care for a person is provided by a wide range of services, from nurseries to nursing homes. Accountants, lawyers, and therapists provide care for money, freedom, and happiness.

---

2 "Why Rolls-Royce Is One British Manufacturer Flying High in a Downturn," *Design Council Magazine* 6 (Summer 2009): 46–47, www.designcouncil.org.uk/Case-studies/DCM-case-studies/Rolls-Royce/; and Irene C. L. Ng, Glenn Parry, Laura A. Smith, Roger Maull, and Gerard Briscoe, "Transitioning from a Goods-Dominant to a Service-Dominant Logic: Visualising the Value Proposition of Rolls-Royce," *Journal of Service Management* 3, forthcoming. Interim location: WMG Service Systems Research Group Working Paper Series, #05/12, ISSN 2049-4297.

Services That Provide Access to People or Things

Many services enable people to use something, or a part of something, temporarily. A railway service provides a seat on a train for a specific journey. A school might offer a child a place in a classroom from the age of 5 to 11. A cinema provides access to a giant screen, a comfy seat, and 90-plus minutes of entertainment. Generally, the services for which access is the primary value are services that give people access to large, complex, or expensive things that they could not obtain on their own.

Other kinds of access services are those that give access to infrastructure over many years. Utilities, such as water, gas, and electricity, are ubiquitous examples in the developed world. The Internet is, of course, a relatively new infrastructure that enables a whole new generation of services that provides access to information, digital media, and technology on a shared basis. Spotify provides access to a huge music library. Google provides access to an enormous database of searches. Facebook provides access to billions of personal pages. In this sense, we can view the Internet as a kind of meta-service, because it enables the provision of many other subservices, which is why so many people insist that no single entity "owns" it.

These services provide individuals with access to large infrastructures that are used in conjunction with many other people. They don't end up owning anything that they can take away and store or give to someone else, apart from the experience they had.

These services are often a fundamental part of people's lives that are typically noticed only when they are disrupted, such as when the daily commuter train is canceled, or when schools are closed due to heavy snow. People expect the infrastructure to always be there for them. As individuals, we understand that we all have our own experiences of the specific access we have to this infrastructure—this is the service layer that enables us to access our bit of the larger whole.

Services That Provide a Response from People or Things

The third category is services that respond to people's (often unforeseen) needs. These services are usually a mix of people and things that are able to assist us: an ambulance rushing to an accident, a teacher helping a child with a math problem, or a store assistant finding a customer a pair of jeans with the right fit. Sometimes these "response" services are anticipated and people buy the right to them in advance through insurance policies, social welfare, or simply by their choice of brand experience.

In many respects, response is the default understanding of what service is—think of a waiter responding to a request for a glass of water, for example. Service is someone doing what he or she has been asked to do. In this sense, response services are fundamentally different from products in that they are not predesigned but created in the moment in reaction to a request.

The three core service values overlap in many instances. An insurance service offers both access to a financial-risk-offsetting infrastructure and a response to a specific issue when a client calls with a claim. A healthcare service provides care on a personal level, but also access to a hospital facility if necessary. It will also transport a patient there in an ambulance if necessary. It is not so much that any one service fits only in one category, but more that the service has different core values at different times.

Making the Invisible Visible

The above examples may well sound obvious. Most people recognize services when they see and experience them, but it is useful to describe and analyze them in this way precisely because services like these are so ubiquitous. It is this very ubiquity that leads them to being taken for granted by both users and providers alike. Thus, they become almost invisible elements of life.

Utilities such as water and electricity are excellent examples of these kinds of services. It is only when there is a power cut or a burst water main that people realize just how dependent they are on these utilities and first start to think about the service infrastructure that is required to provide them. It is because many services are almost invisible that nobody takes care to design them. This is not a conversation we would have if we were talking about a car or a smartphone because the design of these products is quite literally close to the surface and makes up a large proportion of the decision to buy or use them.

As a result, service designers frequently need to make the invisible visible by showing customers what has gone on behind the scenes, showing staff what is happening in the lives of customers, and showing everyone the resource usage that is hidden away. Many of these aspects become part of the business and marketing case for the service (the service proposition).

The Performance of Service

The three core service value categories—care, access, and response—define types of value that services provide to people. Seen in a purely task-fulfilling way, the actual outcome of many services is the same. Renting a car is a good example. Customers can get a car from any car rental company (they hope). Companies may compete on price, and that price may raise or lower expectations of what car and service we might get, but generally prices are similar across the board. The point of difference for any specific service is how it is delivered. We think of this as the performance of the service.

"Performance" is a helpful word, because it means two things: performance as experience and performance as value.

Performance as Experience

Performance, as we understand the word from music or theater, means the style or the way in which the service is delivered. This performance makes up the immediate experiences that service users have, and it is what people often refer to when they describe the service as "good." What they mean is that they liked the way they were treated or the way the service provider performed their tasks. Generally, this is in reference to service staff, such as the front-desk clerk in a hotel or a call center employee.

It is useful to take this concept of performance and expand it from the individual to the overall performance of the entire service organization. If we use a musical metaphor to compare the service to an orchestra or a rock band, we can think of quality of performance in terms of how well all the musicians came together to deliver the music. Music is an interesting metaphor in this regard, because in a band or an orchestra, each musician must play to the best of his or her abilities, yet at the same time play in harmony and keep time with the others. Things can quickly go awry if each musician simultaneously tries to play as a soloist.

We can go a step further to include the qualities that the venue or the support staff brought to the experience. Was the lighting good, and was the sound engineering supporting the experience? This kind of performance is where a service can have its own style—think of an airline such as Virgin, which have gone to great lengths to make the experience of a very rigid flight process different from their competitors by styling the manner, dress, and actions of their inflight team, their digital and print communication, and a host of other touchpoints.

This "experience" aspect of performance is the delivery of the service to the service user on the "front stage." The idea of a music ensemble, harmonious across all aspects of the performance, is critical to services and a concept we will return to when we start examining how to align the complexity of touchpoints that make up service experiences.

Performance as Value

The other meaning of the word "performance," equally useful to service design, is service performance as a measure of value. How well is the service performing? This measure is both outward and inward facing. Outward-facing value measurement asks how well the service is achieving the results promised to the service users. For example, how often does a hip operation result in a 100% recovery? Inward-facing value measurement examines how well the service is performing for the organization. For example, how cost effectively is it delivering hip operations?

This kind of performance is how businesses usually see their activities. Hence, services that we design and they provide will be evaluated in hard performance metrics. Service designers need to design for this aspect of a service as much as for the customer experience.

This value aspect of performance is the "backstage" measure of the service by the business—all the things that happen behind the scenes that help create or run the service experience for customers but that they don't see. This provides a challenge for service designers. We need to be able to measure the cold, hard metrics of the business as well as make the case for measuring the soft and fuzzy aspects of people's experiences. This challenge is discussed in Chapter 8.

Unite the Experience

We doubt we have to preach the value of design to readers of this book, but we all have to make the business case to clients. In our experience, the design approaches described here can be quick, inexpensive, and effective ways to create service experiences that delight customers. Most services involve implementing a complex and usually expensive infrastructure, and our ability to develop quick, cheap prototypes of both products and services early in their development can save organizations enormous amounts of money in sunk investment that may later turn out not to work. Service design aims to unite the experience.

Now, let's look at how.

Summary

- Economies in developed countries have shifted from industrial manufacture to services. The problem is that many companies offering services still think about them with an industrial mindset and try to manage and market services like products.

- A common management approach is to divide an organization into departments, or *silos*. This may lead to each part of the service being well designed, but the real problem is that the entire service has not been designed as a coherent whole. The customer who experiences the whole also experiences the gaps between the touchpoints.

- Many organizations are organized in ways that actually prevent them from delivering good service experiences. The challenge is to redesign both the service and also the culture of the organization.

CHAPTER 3

Understanding People and Relationships

People Are the Heart of Services

Despite the ability of new technologies to automate and augment people's daily lives, people remain at the heart of services. As we mentioned in Chapter 2, a service has no or little intrinsic value until the moment of its use or consumption—services or experiences cannot be stored in a warehouse. But "use" and "consume" are product mindset words and we need to use different language for services. People don't "use" a healthcare professional or a lawyer, and they don't consume a train journey or a stay at a hotel. Instead, people enter into a relationship with professionals and service providers, and their interactions are an act of co-producing the service experience. Thus, we need to think in terms of designing for relationships and experiences that evolve and change over time, rather than just in terms of short moments of consumption or usage.

In the age of self-service Web booking and mobile applications, interpersonal experiences would seem to be on the way out, but services comprise interactions among people, technology, and processes. When these are industrialized and institutionalized, as often happens when organizations grow, they need rehumanization to work properly and connect back to people's human experience of the service. Even human-to-human interactions need this kind of design attention when they are mediated by technology, such as call center interactions or even forms.[1]

It is essential to understand that services are, at the very least, relationships between providers and customers, and more generally, that they are highly complicated networks of relationships between people inside and outside the service organization. The staff who interact with customers are also users and providers of internal services. Most people have tales to tell of how inflexible their IT departments are or how other company policies curb their ability to innovate or provide the service they know their customers want. IT staff respond with stories of how other staff—their "customers"—sap their time with questions and problems that are blindingly obvious (to them). When frontline staff are let down by internal systems and procedures, they become disempowered and inflexible. This is passed down the line and leads to poor customer experiences and service failures.

Industrialization did not just lead to industrial product thinking. We argue that the industrial mode has also led to the stereotypical "faceless corporations" that are often the subject of frustration and poor experiences for service users, because the industrial mindset is usually all about *efficiencies* and economies of scale rather than *effectiveness* of the delivered service. Some customer–provider relationships can end up being toxic and

---

1   See Luke Wroblewski's excellent book, *Web Form Design*, for an insightful analysis of forms as conversations: www.rosenfeldmedia.com/books/webforms/.

combative, and as the history of human warfare shows us, people tend to dehumanize the enemy.

All decisions in an organization stem from people, and in some form or another, other people interact with them and are affected by them. We are more often aware of this with government policy decisions, but the human outcome is frequently overlooked when business discussions include terms such as "consumers" or "target groups," or worse, simply focus on numbers on a spreadsheet.

This industrial mode is inefficient and ineffective for services. As soon as we forget that people—living, feeling, emotive human beings—are involved throughout the entire chain of events, not just at the moment of use by the customer, things go wrong. Organizations can end up being aggressive, manipulative, and aloof, and customers may feel that the only channel available to them for venting their frustration is an unfortunate, underpaid call center employee, who is also bound by rules and regulations and may have had a pretty bad day herself.

The successful businesses and public services of the future will foster a more equal and reciprocal relationship with their customers, one that recognizes the customer as a co-producer of the service.

One of the tools we cover in Chapter 8 simply asks, "How likely is it that you would recommend our company to a friend or colleague?" while another measures the gaps between people's expectations and experiences. It is noticeable here that the main things we are trying to measure are people's relationships to the service and to each other, not efficiency metrics. Services usually involve staff to deliver them, but many are really platforms for creating interactions between other service users. Social networks are, of course, the most high-profile example of this, but some services, such as eBay, are a mix of the two. Issues such as trust, credibility, empathy, and tone of voice are important for many services to thrive. Understanding not just people as individuals but also the relationships they have to others is essential to understanding how a service might operate.

A good example of this relationship building is Zopa, a peer-to-peer lending service that has dramatically altered the customer relationship mode of a financial service. By giving people the ability to network, and by gaining insights into their needs, motivations, and feelings, Zopa is not just another lending and borrowing service. It is a social community with a sense of reciprocal responsibility, something that has certainly been long absent in the mainstream banking world (see Chapter 6 for more on Zopa).

To put people at the heart of services, we need to know who they are. We need to listen to them and obtain accurate information that helps us give them what they need, when they need it. We start by gathering insights.

Insights versus Numbers

Service design draws upon the user- and human-centered design traditions as well as the social sciences to form the basis of our work gathering insights into the experiences, desires, motivations, and needs of the people who use and provide services.

Although the business press makes a lot of noise about "putting customers first," being "customer centered," and having "a customer focus," few organizations employ this form of knowledge with the same rigor that they employ accounting and law. The latter are usually legally mandated for organizations, of course, but developing and maintaining a deep understanding of the people for whom an organization exists to provide value is just as important for the ongoing relevance and survival of a business. Service design is not simply something to add on top of a business proposition after all the numbers have been crunched; it is fundamental to the entire organization and its offerings, and can create a paradigm shift in corporate culture and thinking to one of sustained value and innovation.

All types of organizations have the potential to personalize services and create huge benefits for themselves and their customers. From personalized learning in education to insurance quotes tailored to a policy holder's driving style, personalization is a powerful concept. Shifting attention from the masses to the individual enables radical new opportunities, and because of this fact, service design places more emphasis on qualitative over quantitative research methods.

Service design involves research across all the stakeholders of a project— from the managing director to the end user, and from frontline staff to third-party suppliers. Of course, other disciplines focus on detailed knowledge of customers as a business advantage. The most notable is marketing, and indeed, "insight" is a term widely used in marketing. We are not suggesting that service design is an alternative to marketing, and we acknowledge that service design draws upon a number of disciplines for some of its methods and approaches, but we want to explore how the specific emphasis on design creates value in the experience of services, service propositions, and touchpoints.

Marketing excels in understanding markets and how to reach them through the classic four Ps: price, promotion, product, and place. We are focusing on the fifth P, people, and how we work with people to inform the design of a service.

Market research is typically quantitative and prefers large numbers of respondents. This research can yield some "truths" that are statistically significant and correct, such as the percentage of people who use a certain kind of service (Figure 3.1). This background information can be useful, but discovering through quantitative research that 70% of people do not ride a bicycle (to use a fictional statistic as an example) does not give us any hints about *why* they do not ride bicycles. Statistics are not very actionable for designers—we need to know the underlying reasons.

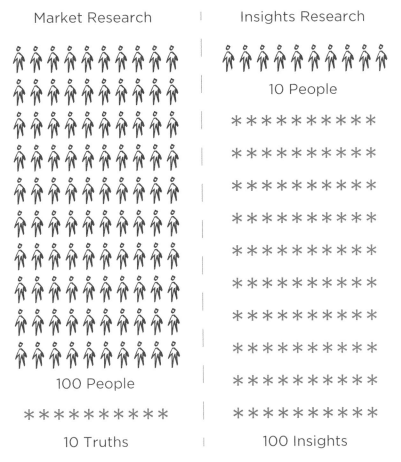

FIGURE 3.1
One is not better than the other, but for our purposes, qualitative research yields more useful insights that we can use as a basis for design than quantitative research's "truths" do.

Qualitative research helps designers dive deeper to understand the chaos and emotions that make us human and behave in seemingly illogical ways. We are interested in people's needs, behaviors, and motivations because these can form the basis of design problems that we try to tackle as designers.

Maybe the non-cyclists in our example prefer the car or bus, or maybe they do not cycle because their city has inadequate bike lanes and the risk of an accident overrides their desire to cycle. If we only work with the statistics, we might assume that the bicycle market is only 30% and decide that it makes more sense to concentrate our efforts on designing better cars and buses. Of course, this choice would likely lead to even fewer bicycle lanes and fewer cyclists. Knowing people's *motivations* for *not* riding bicycles, and understanding the behaviors of those who do, means we might instead focus our design effort on rethinking traffic zoning and bicycle services, as the city of Copenhagen has been doing with great success.[2]

Using Insights to Drive Innovation

Service design and innovation go hand in hand. Much of the work involves shifting clients from an industrial mindset to thinking in a service paradigm. This may mean spending a lot of time helping clients develop an internal culture that will serve them well when it comes to facing future challenges.

Service designers employ the same tools and methods whether they are engaged in innovation work or improvement work, but the purpose of insights is different in each case. By innovation, we mean introducing a new service to a market, or even developing a new market. In this mode, the primary concern is to reduce risk by making sure that the value proposition is viable. The purpose of the research is to generate insight about needs and behaviors that can lay a solid foundation for a productive project and robust ideas, and to confirm these by prototyping early and often to test them out.

Innovation work can be excitingly blue sky and often requires thinking outside of the current norms, but the danger is that it can become distant from people's real needs and problems. We are still waiting for our flying cars and jet packs, and this is probably a good thing because both would most likely result in enormous carbon footprints and crazy sky traffic. If people are asked to dream up their ideal fantasy of transport, they would likely say they would love a flying car or a *Star Trek* transporter. Beyond fulfilling childhood fantasies, however, the underlying *need* of these suggestions is simply an efficient and engaging transportation experience, or even avoiding travel altogether. Innovation brainstorms can easily end up being

---

2 See www.copenhagenize.com, and City of Copenhagen, "Copenhagen—The City of Cyclists," www.kk.dk/sitecore/content/Subsites/CityOfCopenhagen/SubsiteFrontpage/ LivingInCopenhagen/CityAndTraffic/CityOfCyclists.aspx.

driven by technological or marketing fantasies. By asking people about their everyday experiences and observing what they do, how they behave, and what their motivations are, we can ground the innovation process with insights into people's actual lives.

In the end, insights that drive innovation confidently answer the question: "Will our offering make sense in the context of people's lives, and will they find it valuable?"

Many service design projects are about improving an existing service, and here the insights research focus is slightly different. If a service already has many customers, and competitors have entered the market, one can assume that people understand how the service is used and that it is of value. In these cases, the focus is on discovering points of failure in the service (known in service design jargon simply as "fail points") and opportunities for enhancing the experience. This focus means that we can narrow the research scope and look less at unfulfilled needs and more at usage in context. It also means that operational data become a valuable resource and that customer-facing staff are a gold mine for insights. Staff usually can identify most of the problems customers face with a service, although it can be more difficult for them to pinpoint the opportunities for thinking outside the box. When time is short and a service improvement project has a limited budget, it is often a good idea to prioritize the research time with staff and data to dig quickly into the detail that is needed to design great services.

Obviously, these two areas overlap. Improvement may happen through small innovations, or a blue-sky innovation idea may be scaled back and the principles applied to an existing service or touchpoint as an improvement. What changes is the focus of what we are trying get out of the insights research. In either case, the focus is always on people.

Designing with People, Not for Them

People are part of the delivery of services in a way they are not with products. Consumers probably do not know who designed or built their car, for example, but they will have some contact with the person they speak with at a call center or with the nurse who admits them into an emergency ward. We need to design service elements as much for the person who delivers service as we do for the customer.

Service design is about designing *with* people and not just *for* them, and it is here that it differs from classic user-centered design and much of marketing. "People" does not just mean customers or users, it also means the people working to provide the service, often called frontline, front-of-house, or customer-facing staff. Their experience, both in terms of their knowledge and their engagement in the job, is important to the ongoing success of a service for two key reasons.

HourSchool: Engaging Stakeholders in Service Design

by Christina Tran and Jon Kolko

HourSchool is a peer-to-peer learning platform that helps people become teachers. We partnered with Green Doors, a permanent supportive housing community in Austin, Texas, to co-design a peer education program. Green Doors provides housing to more than 300 residents annually, and offers supportive services for those placed in residence. Based on our common values, we committed to creating a strengths-based approach to increase participation and leadership among community residents. HourSchool staff had seen the transformative power of teaching and knew what it took to build a website platform that encouraged peer learning. However, with a community whose main communication channels were offline, a new program needed to be co-designed as a comprehensive service. We needed buy-in, ownership, and engagement throughout the process from all stakeholders—administrative staff, community managers, and residents—so the program would fit into their lives and thrive beyond our involvement.

Using service design as an approach highlighted all the moving parts that needed to work together as a peer education program. As we started to create a service blueprint that outlined key touchpoints, artifacts, and backstage actions, we immediately saw the importance of the community manager's role. Not only would she be spearheading the logistical efforts to organize events, she would also be the one training residents in how they could interact with the service (through templates, requests, and meetings with her). Furthermore, we needed to empower her with the tools to continue making decisions and adjustments to the service blueprint as the program continued to evolve after we left.

From the beginning, we had planned a pilot prototype of the program with multiple rounds of reflection, iteration, and adjustment, so the residents could give feedback and co-create the service along the way. To connect with the community and to start building trust early on, we met casually but continually with people outside of formal research and design sessions. Some of our most valuable insights and design work ended up happening at monthly Resident Council meetings—community meetings where hot issues, such as laundry room complaints or new playground rules, were discussed.

Here are some examples of how showing up to those meetings influenced our service design:

- **Change in perception:** Near the beginning of the process, we introduced an activity about the residents' perception of "classes." We were able to unearth their prejudices about classes as boring lectures and helped them to dream of learning that was social, personalized, and fun. Together we defined event categories of "Lessons," "Demos," and "Socials" and agreed to start planning these for the community. Because they helped to define the language and framework for the new program, residents began to feel ownership in the program rather than like recipients of someone else's ideas.

- **Continuing insights:** We were able to synthesize new insights beyond an initial research phase. The things we heard at the meetings (e.g., computer lab hours were inconsistent) evolved our service blueprint during our working sessions with the community manager (sign-up sheets needed to go to residents as much as we wanted residents to come to the sign-up sheets we posted in the computer lab).

- **Empathy:** We got to know people's names, and people got to know ours. During the meetings, we saw firsthand the complexity of people's lives and the number of things competing for their attention. We were continually reminded that our peer education program was just one slice of the larger pie. This drove us to make our service as relevant as possible by aligning it with people's goals (both staff and residents) and by connecting our program to other parts of the system in meaningful ways.

Over time, the meetings themselves became a touchpoint in our peer education program because of their consistency in community life. Announcing new classes, soliciting requests, and recruiting volunteer organizers are now standing agenda items. In the end, one of the most rewarding benefits of attending the monthly meetings was witnessing the changes firsthand as components of our peer education program took root. As people shared fun stories from attending classes, the meetings became a place where residents could inspire and encourage each other to take the leap, reach for a goal, and support each other along the way.

Christina Tran is the program design lead at HourSchool. She is a human-centered designer who combines service and interaction design methods with practices from community management, program development, and social entrepreneurship.

Jon Kolko is the founder and director of the Austin Center for Design, a progressive educational institution teaching interaction design and social entrepreneurship. His most recent book is Wicked Problems: Problems Worth Solving *(Austin Center for Design, 2012).*

First, in very simple terms, happy staff equals happy customers, so their inclusion in the design of services ensures that providing the service will be a positive experience. Staff who are involved in the creation and improvement of service not only feel more engaged but through learning about the complex ecology of the service they provide and how to make use of innovation tools and methods, they are also able to continually improve the service themselves.[3] Service innovation should have a life span beyond the length of time the service designers are involved in the project. This means recognizing that other stakeholders may engage in many of the activities of service design as part of a continual process of change.

Second, along with customers, frontline staff are often the real experts. They provide insights into the potential for service design that are frequently as valuable to the project as insights from customers, and they can provide a perspective on the day-to-day experiences that managers and marketing people may never experience.

Working across Time and Multiple Touchpoints

For designers who come from a discipline that already uses human-centered design methods, much of this material will be familiar. Understanding people and their daily lives and needs provides the central insights on which many design projects are built (in an ideal world). The difference between service design and product or UX design, for example, is that the number of stakeholders we are designing for is usually larger, the number and range of touchpoints broader, and all of these interact over time.

Segmentation by Journey Stage versus Target Groups

In our definition of service design, we talk about experiences that happen over time. It is relatively simple to gain insight about an experience that happens in a short amount of time, such as an online purchase or a patient's consultation with a doctor, but how do we gain insight into experiences that change and evolve over years or even decades?

In product design or marketing research, we would typically segment the market and interview people in different age, socioeconomic, or behavioral groups. In services, a more useful way to engage with people is by looking at *different stages of their relationship with the service.* This strategy allows us to research the different journeys people might take through a service and how they transition through the various touchpoints.

---

3 This alignment of employee and customer satisfaction is known as the "satisfaction mirror"; see J. L. Heskett, W. E. Sasser, and L. A. Schlesinger, *The Service Profit Chain*, 1st ed. (New York: Free Press, 1997).

Unlike many products or screen-based interfaces, services do not lend themselves to lab testing. For a start, services usually involve large infra-structures, and it would be difficult to test a complete train journey without a rail network infrastructure, although we can prototype elements of it. More important, people interact with services through different channels in different situations that often include interactions with other people. Context is critical to gathering insights into people's interactions with touchpoints, and a lab is not a context in which this can happen (unless the project involves scientists).

For example, one day a customer might buy a train ticket online, another day from a counter in the station, and the next day from a ticket machine or on the train. In addition, the ticket-purchasing experience is closely connected to pricing, route, and departure information, the signage in a station, how staff deal with questions, and the quality of the train ride itself. Third-party services that connect to the train ride also play important roles, such as buses and taxis, credit cards, maps, cleaning services, and the café where travelers can comfortably wait and grab a bite to eat.

From a service point of view, we are really after understanding how different touchpoints work together to form a complete experience. Therefore, try to do research with people in the situations where they use the service. Study how people use a service at home, on the road, and at work, and then connect the dots.

In addition to looking for latent and explicit needs and desires, as is commonly done in most design projects, also look closely for service-specific insights. Look for touchpoints that may be missing but are needed to create a good experience, or touchpoints that are superfluous. Look for situations in which the service could play a more valuable role, or instances when it is smart to keep people from noticing that it is there.

What is most important to look for is variation in quality between the touch-points and the gap between expectations and experiences. When people get what they expect, they feel that the quality is right. Whether it is a premium or a low-cost service, a minimal gap between expectation and experience means greater customer satisfaction.

All of this can be much more difficult than it sounds and can get very complex very quickly. There are natural and economic limits to what we are able to influence, and if we try to track every touchpoint, we will end up trying to re-create the world. A car-sharing experience might happen in the context of a city, so we might want to look at parking spaces, which means we end up dealing with city government, and before long we are wrestling with the entire country's traffic infrastructure policy. Thus, it is important to be strategic and decide on the scope of your insights research. The grumpy café owner in the train station is probably not a touchpoint that we can work on if our client is the rail company, although we might try to find out why the owner is so grumpy and ruins travelers' days (perhaps the rent the rail company charges him is too high). On the other hand, he might have wonderful insights into travelers' confusions because he gets asked where the station exit is several times a day.

Summary

- People are part of the delivery of services in a way they are not with products. The value of a service is closely linked to the quality of relationships between providers and customers, as well as the networks of relationships between people inside and outside the service organization.

- We need to design service elements as much for the person who delivers the service as for the customer. This means designing *with* people and not just *for* them.

- To design for people, we need insights into people's needs, motivations, and behaviors. Qualitative research can usually provide the data for these insights better than quantitative research.

- It is important to research people's activities and interactions across all the touchpoint channels as well as the segments of their journey through the service.

CHAPTER 4

Turning Research into Insight and Action

The process of gathering insights draws on a range of research methodologies, specifically design, usability, and ethnographic methods. Those familiar with UX design, human-centered design, and product and social design projects will be familiar with many of these methods. This chapter describes how these methods are used in the context of service design as well as why and when we use them.

Most designers work in commercial contexts in which budgets and time are generally pressured. Although it is important to try to bring as much rigor to your research process as possible—not least because it helps prove the business case for it—the goal is not necessarily published research. The goal is usable insight that will improve the quality of the service design projects you are working on. It is essential to realize that any insight is better than none and that insight can become addictive. Once your colleagues and clients have a taste, they will come back for more to validate or prototype your initial assumptions.

So where do you start? The answer is, as ever, "It depends." Instead of preaching an ideal process that you are unlikely to have the chance to fully execute, the following approaches and examples are grouped into realistic levels and scenarios. This framework will help you think about how to generate insights that will fit the current needs of your team and the business, and it is a good starting point for those new to service design.

Levels of Insights

Regardless of the arguments you make for its power to generate insights, research is often time consuming and thus expensive. Convincing a new client to commit to a large research budget up front and trust that you will come up with something useful may be a stretch. The process is always the age-old trade-off between time, money, and quality. A useful way to think about this is to have a menu of low, middle, and high levels of detail (and effort) to draw from as the situation requires.

Low—What They Say

The low granularity of analysis is basically a summary of what a small sample of around four or five research participants say in relatively short depth interviews (say, 45 minutes), and does not include any other activities, such as in-person observation, workshops, site visits, or testing. Costs include recruitment expenses and any participant incentive. This level of research is unlikely to include a travel budget, so the interviews may need to be conducted in the local area or by telephone or e-mail.

The output produced for the client is a brief executive summary and the top five observations from the depth interviews delivered as a PDF document or in a short presentation. The observations provide some possible quick wins for the client.

Middle—What We Saw

The middle level of analysis provides deeper and more crafted insights based on research with around 10 participants. This deeper level may be of benefit to clients who require the research to have some long-term value beyond a specific project or who need to share it with a bigger group within the company.

The output provides top insights plus a summary, but is more in-depth than the low level of analysis (Figure 4.1). This middle level also prioritizes issues for the project, which are produced from an internal workshop with the client that is conducted by the service design agency. The insights findings may be presented as a written report, presentation slides, a blog, or summary boards (see "Collating and Presenting Your Insights" below for more details).

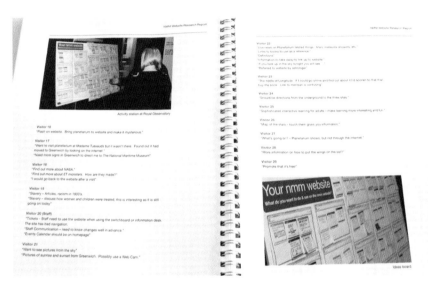

FIGURE 4.1
An example of a middle-level insights report.

High—What It Means

A highly detailed level of analysis requires more depth interviews and a combination of other insights techniques to generate the data. The analysis in this level is much deeper and more systematic, and includes more about what the insights mean strategically for the industry and the client's project, along with suggested recommendations and solutions for the client. The output can also be more varied, including those from the low and middle variants, but may extend to a short video or a workshop with the client and/or other stakeholders to share and build on the insights gained through the initial research.

Insights-Gathering Methods

Many of the insights-gathering methods described in this section are drawn from ethnography, but it is important to note that, although we are using ethnographic methods and techniques, we are not doing proper ethnography in its own right. Ethnography is a term that has had some use and abuse by designers over the past few years in the sense of "Yeah, we did some ethnography and then got on with the design work." Ethnography has a history, approach, and rigor that is much more loosely interpreted for design research, and when we borrow its methodology, we should be respectful of how and why it was developed in the first place—to understand and document the knowledge, relationships, and beliefs of social or cultural groups, often through long-term participant observation of a year or more. Of course, the ideal scenario is to hire a trained ethnographer to work with the design researchers and design team.

Although the following methods are commonly used by those working on service design projects, this list is not exhaustive. Any methods that help you understand people's motivations and behaviors more deeply, including those methods you may already be using in interaction or UX work, will contribute to a service design project.

Depth Interviews

Depth interviews are long, in-context interviews that tend to be fairly open in their structure. They are an inspiring and productive way of generating insights into an individual's perceptions, behaviors, and needs. They are also good for uncovering values, opinions, explicit and latent information, interactions, and idea inspiration. These interviews are usually guided by a theme, and they provide an opportunity to explore relevant issues in depth with participants, query and verify what they say, and achieve consensus on what they mean. The results of depth interviews compare very favorably with those from focus groups and are less expensive to undertake. Angus Jenkinson, director of the Centre for Integrated Marketing at the University of Bedfordshire Business School, argues that focus groups are structurally problematic because each member gets only a few minutes to speak and even these short interactions are influenced by social pressures. In contrast, in-depth interviews offer deeper insights and are better value for the money.[1]

Interviews are the most efficient way to engage with people in their own context and allow them to explain how they see things. This means using a number of techniques to make interviews as engaging, informal, and as interactive as possible through drawing and other creative activities. An engaging interview is the key to a productive rapport.

---

[1] See Angus Jenkinson, "Austerity Marketing and Fat Insights," July 25, 2008, www.stepping-stones.org/Blog/?p=3.

Meet participants in their own homes or places of work to bring ethnographic context to the interview (Figure 4.2). If you want to learn about how people carry out their activities in the workplace, for example, interviewing them at home will be of limited use. When in the context of their workplace, however, many visual prompts will be present that can help direct the conversation, and you can take photographs or film the things the participant is talking about. Workplace interviews have some limitations, however, which are discussed in "Business-to-Business Depth Interviews" below.

FIGURE 4.2
A depth interview in the participant's home environment.

Encourage other members of the design team to attend and engage so they can share the experience of meeting users and discovering insights. Occasionally, you may want to ask clients to attend the interviews, too, but this can be a double-edged sword. Clients will obtain a greater understanding of the methods and project results, and they are often energized and excited when hearing this feedback firsthand, but they need to be prepared to remain passive. Some clients can manage this, but others want to jump in and correct a participant's misunderstanding of their brand or product, which closes down the participant's range of responses very quickly and skews the outcome of the interview. In some cases, even the presence of a person representing the company can close down participants' responses, but it might equally give frustrated users a sense of being heard and encourage them to open up and vent about all of the things that have annoyed them. However, interviewees should never be corrected about something they are explaining, even if they are completely wrong. Instead, ask them how or why they know what they are saying; it will reveal a lot more.

The way participants tell their own stories provides researchers with a rich resource for identifying how they perceive and articulate the subject. Priorities and embellishments are helpful indicators of what is valuable to them, so rather than impose structure, use a loose interview guide to ensure you cover the themes and material you need, and then coax out detail and verify that you have understood their perspective. Depth interviews differ from other methods because they allow the time to uncover this level of detail. They may range from around 45 minutes (probably the shortest usable time, unless you have only a tiny window of time with an expert or top manager) to two or three hours, especially if you are asking someone to show you around his or her home or workplace.

Variations on the Depth Interview

Two other types of depth interview are focused more on specific questions than the open interviews described above: consumer interviews in pairs and business-to-business (B2B) interviews. They differ slightly in terms of what you are trying or able to discover and in terms of the interpersonal dynamics and structure.

Interviewing Consumers in Pairs

For some people, a one-to-one interview can feel imposing and exposing, although a good interviewer should be able to put them at ease quickly. In one-to-one situations, consumers in particular may say what they think you want to hear. For this reason, we find consumer research interviews conducted with couples or pairs of friends can be more useful than interviews with individuals because the subjects feed off each other's answers and build on them. If they know each other well, they are likely to feel more comfortable and give genuine answers. We have found that pairs provide the most truthful feedback, and of course, you get two people's opinions in the same time it takes to interview one person. In this respect, pairs represent the best value for the client.

One thing to be careful of is when one person puts opinions in the mouth of the other. This usually happens with couples in long-term relationships more than with friends. A husband might explain to the interviewer that his wife hates a particular TV show or that she knows nothing about how their home entertainment equipment is set up, for example. The dynamics of the relationship might mean that she does not contradict this statement during the interview, even if it is not true. Even if it *is* true, if it is part of the research topic, you will want to find out *why* she does not like a particular show. Perhaps the reason is that her husband always complains loudly when it is on, and it has nothing to do with the show itself. On the other hand, the wife might also contradict her husband by revealing that he has no idea how the home entertainment system works either. We have experienced this kind of "he said/she said" thing in more than one interview over the years.

As Ben Scales from the Association for Qualitative Research says, "Friendship or family cells provide a natural form of censorship. After all, it's hard to exaggerate about your behavior when you've got someone sitting next to you who knows you well."[2]

Children or teenagers tend to feel uncomfortable when interviewed on their own (and conducting such interviews may be considered inappropriate in some cultures and contexts), so you are better off interviewing them in pairs. Be aware, however, that they will almost certainly try to impress each other, especially at certain ages (teenage boys, for example).[3]

Business-to-Business Depth Interviews

One-to-one depth interviews are best used in B2B situations or when interviewing client stakeholders. You may be interviewing business customers or suppliers of your client. In a one-to-one context, they are more likely to tell you things about their company that they might not say in front of their colleagues or superiors. Also, B2B interviews can be difficult to set up if more than one person is involved because their schedules may conflict with each other's and with yours.

Interviewing or observing people at their place of work is useful, especially if you are interested in the workplace context and their workflow, but if you are asking people to talk openly about their feelings about their job, then B2B interviews may be better conducted in a neutral environment, such as a coffee shop. People may not be comfortable talking about work in their home, and they may not be as open and honest if interviewed in the workplace.

Sometimes you have no choice about where or with whom you conduct interviews. Some insight from an interview conducted in less than optimal conditions is usually better than none at all, unless it really appears to be contradictory or the conditions have skewed the responses too much. In the end, field researchers cannot avoid these elements, just as they cannot completely jettison their own cultural baggage and interpretations. Most people think they can be objective, but this is an illusion. Sometimes you just do not develop a rapport with interviewees or their views are so different from yours that it is hard not to react negatively, even if only through unconscious body language. Due to a last-minute scheduling change, Andy once found himself interviewing a group of lawyers from an oil exploration company about hydrogen fuel cell transportation options for the future. Needless to say, the atmosphere was not particularly open and jovial. The best that you can do in these situations is to be aware of these influences and

---

2 Ben Scales, "Creative Elevation," Association for Qualitative Research, 2008, www.aqr.org.uk/inbrief/document.shtml?doc=ben.scales.14-01-2008.elevation.

3 See Kay Tisdall, John Davis, and Michael Gallagher, *Researching with Children and Young People: Research Design, Methods and Analysis* (London: Sage Publications, 2009) for a good reference guide in this area.

take them into account when making interpretations of the transcripts and other data, or to simply thank the interviewees and end the interviews early.

Preparing for Interviews

Indi Young's *Mental Models* has a very good section on setting up interviews, with detailed advice about working out who to recruit and dealing with research participant recruitment agencies.[4] Below is a general overview of the process that we usually follow.

- **Recruit:** This step can take two to three weeks, so it should be started early. If possible, use a recruitment company to do the hard work of recruiting interviewees. This may seem expensive but saves a lot of time. You need to be as clear as possible with the recruiters about who you need. More unusual participants (such as farriers or specific medical patients) may need to be sourced with the client's help. You can also use your own (real or virtual) social networks to interview friends of friends. This can help create an instant level of trust with someone who is still essentially a stranger.

- **Research:** You may not know much about the topic you are interviewing on. If this is the case, you may need to research the area, but don't spend too much time on it. Sometimes it is best to be a little naïve because it prevents you from making assumptions; otherwise, you will have to learn to ask deliberately naïve questions.

- **Plan the topics:** When you have found out more, construct a prompt card. This should be a list of topics you want to cover during the interview, not a strict list of specific questions. The interview should be a conversation, not an interrogation.

- **Design the tools:** Design appropriate paper activities to make the interview more engaging and interactive (see "Probes and Tools" below).

- **Prepare:** Think through the details of going out to do the depth interviews (see "Practicalities of Conducting Insights Research" below).

Participant Observation

Participant observation, or shadowing, provides rich, in-depth, and accurate insights into how people use products, processes, and procedures. It is very useful for understanding context, behavior, motivations, interactions, and the reality of what people do, rather than what they say they do. It gives good depth and insight into latent needs—the things people actually need, but perhaps do not know that they need because they are so used to their old routine.

---

4 Indi Young, *Mental Models: Aligning Design Strategy with Human Behavior* (New York: Rosenfeld Media, 2008), www.rosenfeldmedia.com/books/mental-models/.

Observation is usually quite time consuming in comparison to other insights methods and can be difficult to arrange because someone must be prepared to have you accompany them for a few hours or a full day. In some situations, such as shadowing someone trying to find their way around a public transit system, this method is not too invasive. In workplace situations, it can be trickier because a sales representative may not want you sitting there while he or she is in a meeting with a customer, or people may be uncomfortable discussing confidential information in front of you, even if you have signed a nondisclosure agreement.

Short observations are a useful starting point when the team is not familiar with the area being researched. They give you a sense of the atmosphere and environment in which people are carrying out activities (e.g., buying, selling, giving a diagnosis, receiving treatment). They can also give you a good sense of activity flows (e.g., new patients' names are written on the whiteboard and entered into the computer, and a blue file is used to mark their nonemergency status). Longer, in-depth observations can be used to uncover fresh insights into even familiar activities. Sometimes the fact that a task is very commonly carried out can blind people to the opportunities for improvement.

It is essential with this type of research to carry out the observations in the participant's natural environment, such as an office, home, or in the context of an activity, such as trying to find the right train across town (Figure 4.3). Otherwise, you will have nothing to observe, or you will be observing tasks out of their usual context.

FIGURE 4.3
Participant observation on Norway's transport system.

The goals of participant observation depend on who the participant is, whether a customer or a business. Observing customers means observing people in their everyday lives. This method is useful when working with customers to uncover how they use and engage with products and services. Observing the participant in a professional role is often done when working with clients to help uncover how their internal procedures can be improved.

When observing, there are two approaches you can take: the fly-on-the-wall method in which you just observe and pretend not to be there, or a more active approach in which you interact with users by asking them questions about what they are doing. People do all sorts of strange and wonderful things when they work or use something, and they often have developed their own workarounds for problems with a system, service, or interface. Even if you think you can see their rationale, it helps to act a little naïve and ask them to explain what they are doing and why.

Preparing for Participant Observation

Here are some steps to follow when planning participant observations.

- **Recruit:** Arranging these sessions can be tricky because you are intruding into someone's life and workflow. You don't want to get in the way or miss anything, so good planning is essential and you need to be sure to find the best candidate in the organization for your research goals.

- **Set expectations:** Make sure you understand what the client wants from the insights activity so that you are aware of what to look out for when observing. This understanding will also help with analysis. Create a list of questions that you want answered to serve as a guide for what to watch for. At the same time, it is important to remain open to whatever presents itself during the observation period. You don't want to miss something interesting because you have your nose buried in your notes.

- **Design the tools:** To record the activity, you may want to create some paper activities for you or the participant to complete (discussed in "Probes and Tools" below).

- **Prepare:** Each observation activity is unique, so preparation is important. Think about what you should wear and how you will record what you observe. Decide how much time you will need to spend in observation to obtain the information you require.

FIGURE 4.4
Becoming the user or a member of the client's staff for a day is an enlightening way to gain user insights. Don't forget to dress the part as Natalie McGhee and Sean Miller have done here.

Participation—Becoming the User

Participation is a very involved but enlightening way to gain user insights. It is not just a way to study or document the user's lifestyle or occupation, but allows you to become part of the user group you are researching (Figure 4.4).

Participation can provide researchers with a unique, firsthand understanding of the way users feel and behave, and it is an excellent strategy for developing empathy and asking questions clients might not think of. Researchers can experience things for themselves that may be hard for someone to describe to them.

We encourage clients to try the participation technique of becoming their own customers. This helps them empathize with their customers and allows them to uncover insights and ideas for improvement for themselves, not just hear it secondhand from us. For many clients, this activity can be quite daunting, but it can also be an exciting and engaging experience for them. The client-as-customer approach can also be done with the service safari described below.

Participation activities can be as simple as being a mystery shopper or as complex as getting a job with the client to experience being a new employee. When it is not possible to literally become your users—because they have a disability, for example—you can simulate the experience. To feel what it is like to use a service's touchpoints as an elderly person, you could wear an "aging suit" made up of heavy gloves to simulate stiffness and loss of dexterity in the hands, a helmet/visor to limit vision, and other elements to restrict movement.[5] You can spend the day in a wheelchair to see what it is like to go shopping or use public transportation.[6]

Preparing for Participation

Here are a few specific tips to bear in mind when planning to use the participation method.

- **Be open:** You may have to do things you haven't done before; it is important to be open and embrace them. You want to avoid distracting the people you are studying by having them look after you.

- **Be organized:** Good planning is essential. You are about to wade into someone else's workspace and workflow. You are also likely to be representing your client to the public or your client's customers. Treat what you are doing with the same respect you would show any real job. Some things will happen spontaneously, so have everything you need to document the situation at hand.

- **Document:** Choose the most suitable method for recording the task you are carrying out. Do not insist on sticking a camera in someone's face when discreet note taking would be more appropriate.

Service Safaris

A service safari gives participants—usually members of the project team from the client side—firsthand experience of other (sometimes seemingly unrelated) services (Figure 4.5). Participants use these other services for a few hours or even a day. Some of the services to be explored should be outside the client's own industry, which enables participants to be more objective about how the services they experience are delivered. This experience may provide ideas that they can transfer back to their own business.

---

5   To simulate aging, MIT's AgeLab developed a complex suit called AGNES (Age Gain Now Empathy System); see http://agelab.mit.edu/agnes-age-gain-now-empathy-system.

6   David McQuillen told a great story about the power of his team's "immersion" approach in his presentation at euroGel 2006, when he was Director of Customer Experience at Credit Suisse. The video is available at http://vimeo.com/3720227.

FIGURE 4.5
A service safari allows you or your client to experience being a
customer of another service and try out a range of different experiences, both good and bad.

A service safari can help stimulate clients to enlarge, shift, and reframe the
way they think about serving their customers because they are seeing themselves as the service user instead of the service provider. This empathy for
their customers will help innovate fresh ideas. It is an excellent technique
to use when redesigning an existing service and can prove valuable when
designing a new service because it helps inspire new service ideas.

Service safaris are usually best used in conjunction with a workshop or
sketching session. This helps clients translate what they have learned from
the safari into ideas for their business and provides inspiring material to
kick off those sessions. It can be a great icebreaker for teams just starting to
get to grips with service design.

Planning a service safari can be time consuming. Here are some points to consider.

- **Budget:** Service safaris can be expensive, so it is important to agree on a budget with the client before organizing anything.

- **Research:** Choose the services you want the clients to experience. We usually go for a mix of services that we think will be really good or really bad (but these can be surprising).

- **Plan:** After deciding which services the clients should try, you may need to book these activities. Draw up a clear schedule of what each client will do on the safari. Participants should be provided with the money needed to pay for the activities on their service safari, and they should be sent out on their own (individually or in groups), but not with members of the service design team.

- **Prepare the tools:** Each group on the safari should be provided with tools to document each service, typically a camera and a journal, perhaps one prepared ahead of time with pointers on what to look out for or with a specific structure for notes.

- **Debrief:** When the participants come back from the safari, they should present their findings and create a list of good and bad aspects of the services. This can be the first activity of a workshop.

User Workshops

Focus groups can be full of people telling you what they think you want to hear or who are influenced by others in the group, so you might prefer to do co-design user workshops. Encourage pairs of friends to attend, as they are likely to be more comfortable with this dynamic and more truthful in their answers. These kinds of workshops are a great way to quickly produce large numbers of insights and ideas.

Use probe-like tasks (see "Probes and Tools" below) in these workshops to warm up participants and start generating useful discussion (Figure 4.6). These tasks can help less dominant participants, who may not be comfortable speaking in front of a group, express themselves through another medium. Encourage participants to develop their own ideas, and use sketching or collage making to help people get out of their normal, verbal mode of thinking.

FIGURE 4.6
User workshops are a good alternative to focus groups.

Preparing for a User Workshop

When planning to conduct a user workshop, here are a few tips to consider.

- **Recruit:** It can take two to three weeks to set up a workshop, so recruit early. You should try to recruit friendship pairs or couples rather than individuals. Groups of 4 to 16 people are ideal for a user workshop.

- **Prepare the venue:** Arrange a suitable venue for the workshop that is large and comfortable enough for everyone to work on the activities. Sometimes participant recruiters can assist with finding a suitable space. Arrange for food and beverages, if required. Offering food before a workshop is scheduled to begin can help get participants there on time. If the venue has little wall area, you may want to take along some foam-core or display boards to use as temporary post-up spaces.

- **Create a schedule:** Draw up a realistic timetable of what will be done and when. You will almost certainly run out of time for all the things you have planned, at least the first few times you conduct a workshop. Be prepared to skip over some activities and be clear about which ones are more important than others. It is useful to have a backup plan, just in case.

- **Design the tools:** Spend some time designing the tools required to engage people in the activities. Make sure you have enough copies of any worksheets, as well as plenty of pens, pencils, markers, glue sticks, scissors, sticky notes, masking tape, and any other tools you might need, such as building blocks or modeling clay.

- **Document:** The client may want documentation of the workshop. Video is sometimes requested, but usually photos and the materials produced in the workshop are enough. If you do need to film the workshop and you are the facilitator, ask someone else from your team to do the recording. You will not have time to attend to this task properly *and* facilitate well. A simple approach is to set up a camera on a tripod in one place and just record any presentations given by the groups.

Probes and Tools

Probes and tools are useful aids for the insights research approaches described above. Using only verbal inputs during interviews or workshops can be limiting. Some people can describe or envisage their world, thoughts, feelings, and relationships better through images, diagrams, sketches, and activities.

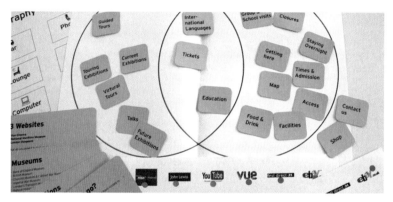

FIGURE 4.7
Depth interview probes from a project for the National Maritime Museum.

Probes are task-based insights activities that are good for generating insights with minimum influence from the researcher and bringing out views in quieter participants (Figure 4.7). These are more formally called *cultural probes*, as developed by Bill Gaver of the Royal College of Art.[7]

Probes can be used during an interview session to engage participants, or they can be left with interviewees to complete over time. Sometimes it is useful to leave a probe task with users to gain insight into other parts of their lives or to record an event that happens over time and cannot be studied in an interview situation.

---

7   See Bill Gaver, Tony Dunne, and Elena Pacenti, "Design: Cultural Probes," *interactions* 6, no. 1 (1999): 21–29.

Preparing Probes and Tools

Probes can be personalized according to the client's requirements. Probes can take some time to define, so it is best to look at what has already been done for inspiration. Below are some examples of what we have developed and used in the past, but it is by no means an exhaustive list. Plenty of examples of cultural probes and other interview aids can be found online and in the literature. Consider them as tools for your research toolbox and add to your collection as you come across or develop more over the years. Roberta Tassi's Service Design Tools website (www.servicedesigntools.org) is a great place to share them, too.

The tools that you use most frequently for interviews and workshops can be assembled in travel kits ahead of time. If you replenish the kits after each session, you will have everything you need for the next session and be less likely to forget something important.

Events Timelines and Journey Maps

Timelines are used to record an event or journey experienced by a person or group over time. You can set it up as a simple continuum with the present day in the middle and a certain amount of time—weeks, months, years—on either side, depending on your goal. For example, you could ask people to map their vacation travel over a period of 10 years to get a sense of their changing lifestyles (Figure 4.8), or ask people to map their health over time. Asking participants to look back over time usually helps them make more realistic predictions about their future needs and wishes, and it can help them highlight present needs and worries. This can be done with individuals on a single sheet of paper (a prepared template is helpful), but you can also create one as a group using sticky notes on the wall, allowing you to gather insights into the history of a group or organization as well as where they want to head in the future.

Events Timeline/Journey Map

Travel Timeline Record travel/holidays. Where did you go ? Why did you go? What were the highlights? What were the problems?

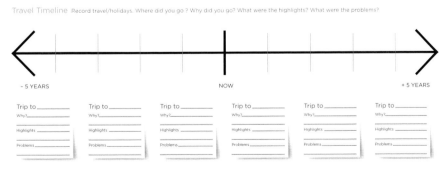

FIGURE 4.8
A timeline for mapping tourism experiences over a 10-year period.

Diaries

Diaries are used to ask people to document an event or period of time. These can be done in paper format, as voice recordings, or as a video diary. You can also ask people to include photographs alongside their writing. Diaries often reveal more intimate thoughts and feelings about people's lives—more than they might tell you in an interview. A student of Andy's had great success with diaries in a project about the loved ones of dementia sufferers. Although it was too upsetting to talk about in an interview, one participant wrote down some very moving insights in her diary about her and her husband's social life as his signs of Alzheimer's disease started to show. The downside of this kind of self-documentation is that you only get what participants want you to see or what they think is important, and unless you interview them again later, you cannot ask follow-up questions about specific points.

Diaries can take structured or open forms. You can put together a list of things you want people to self-document, such as writing down the time and details of their usage of a mobile device (Figure 4.9). Or you can leave them to write what they want in a blank notebook. The structured form helps you compare and collate the data, but the open form gives you more qualitative personal detail (that will probably be more work to analyze).

If you have the time and budget, it is helpful to put together a custom diary for participants. It can be as simple as applying a sticker to an off-the-shelf notebook, or creating a spiral-bound booklet made up of templates you have printed out. Your effort in putting together attractive, professional materials will be recognized by participants, and they will likely take your project more seriously.

FIGURE 4.9
People often reveal more intimate thoughts and feelings about their lives in diaries than they would give in interviews. This structured diary, for a research project by Swisscom, is a record of the participant's mobile device usage.

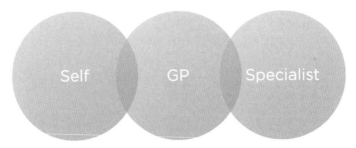

FIGURE 4.10
Venn diagrams are a useful way of getting people to visually group together activities or behaviors. This one asks participants to assign healthcare issues to themselves, their general practitioner (GP), or a specialist in order to understand how people relate to health services.

Venn Diagrams

Venn diagrams are a useful tool in interviews and workshops because they can be adapted to many different subjects. They are a way of getting people to visually group together activities or behaviors (Figure 4.10). For example, you can use Venn diagrams to ask what participants do or do not feel comfortable doing on the Internet, who they go to for healthcare advice, or what information should be on various sections of a website.

You can either bring a template prepared in advance or simply draw one on a blank sheet of paper; one advantage is that no graphic design skills are needed to create them. If you create a large one to hang on the wall, a group of people can post items within the circles on sticky notes. This exercise promotes discussion and allows participants to move items around.

With Venn diagrams, you must have sets that make sense to overlap with each other, otherwise the middle section will never get filled in. The overlapping area often reveals the sweet spot of the project's focus.

Brand Sheets

A brand sheet is a simple tool and it is one that is always worth having in your bag or on your laptop for interviews. It is simply a sheet of logos of different products and services (Figure 4.11). The idea is to uncover what brands people use, the choices they make, and why. Sometimes people forget about all the goods and services they use or how they feel about them. They might use some brands only a few times a year, whereas others are so ubiquitous that people do not give them any thought. Visual material, such as logos or key brand touchpoints (listing magazines they read, websites they use, shops they visit, and so on), act as discussion prompts and generate great insights. You can bet that at least one of the logos will prompt a rant or a customer experience story from each participant.

FIGURE 4.11

A brand sheet can help elicit responses about people's relationships to the more abstract services they may use.

Probe Cameras

A disposable camera is an essential part of a cultural probe kit (Figure 4.12). A camera can be given to a user with a list of instructions about what to photograph, sometimes with a request to write accompanying notes. If you create a custom cardboard wrapper with instructions printed on the back, participants will not have to fiddle around with an extra sheet of paper. The instructions may ask the participants to photograph their desk, their home, recycling bins, someone they admire, their last meal, the last item they purchased, and so on.

FIGURE 4.12
Disposable cameras with custom covers ready to be sent out to participants in a research project.

Camera probes, like diaries, are useful because people will photograph intimate things or activities that they might not have let an interviewer photograph. Cameras can also be very useful when it is not cost effective to send a researcher to do observations. You can send out a kit to the participants instead.

If participants need to return the cameras by mail, don't forget to provide a stamped and addressed envelope. If you don't want to wait for the disposable cameras to be developed, you can provide a set of cheap digital cameras or ask people to use their mobile phones.

Given the ubiquity of smartphones, most of which have good cameras, you can simply ask people to take a series of photos with their phones and e-mail them to you or post them online. The advantage is that you can ask a lot of people to take part via e-mail. The disadvantage is that it is less structured (the photos might be posted in any order, whereas a film camera has a fixed sequence) and it is easy for people to forget or only do half of the task. Most people like to have a special object in their hands and will make more of an effort if you have done so from your side by providing the camera.

Photograph Lists

Photograph lists are often used when going on insights interviews (Figure 4.13). It is always good to take pictures of interviewees and their homes or environment to create context when writing up and presenting interviews. When you sit down together to go over a neutral list, people are more comfortable saying what they do and do not want you to photograph. It is easier to gain permission to take photographs of things this way because people are social animals and tend to want to help a researcher fulfil a task they have been set by someone else. If you just ask for permission verbally, you are more likely to be perceived as just being personally nosey.

Photography

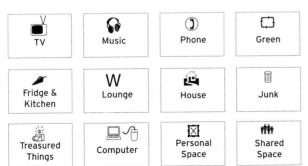

FIGURE 4.13
Showing participants a list of items you would like to photograph gives them the opportunity to state up front what they are comfortable with, and makes it seem less like you are just being nosey.

Visual Interpretations

Sometimes participants can be more expressive when drawing a visual interpretation of something than they can be with words (Figure 4.14). The fact that drawing is trickier for some also helps participants get out of their normal verbal arguments and routines. This technique is great for young children and for getting participants to express their emotions. It is important to make sure people do not feel pressure to "draw well" and that they understand any kinds of doodles or style are more than okay. The drawings can make excellent artifacts when presenting the results of your research.

FIGURE 4.14
Drawings and doodles allow participants to be more expressive than they might be with words. This participant—Samuel Frei, a former student of Andy's—was particularly good at sketching the way he thought about his bank card, but even simple, rough sketches can get the point across.

Item Labels

Participants can be given tags or labels with instructions to use them to point out objects within their homes that have particular attributes, such as "most treasured" or "impulse purchase." You can even provide first-, second-, and third-prize rosettes and ask people to rank objects in their home according to particular criteria (Figure 4.15). The idea behind all of these labels is to start a conversation about why an object is thought of in a particular way. You will soon find that participants start telling stories about their possessions and, through this process, their personal values and beliefs will become apparent.

FIGURE 4.15
Asking participants to attach tags or labels to items that are important to them can stimulate conversation. This participant gave his computer monitor a "1st Place" rosette. (Photograph by Lea Tschudi)

Practicalities of Conducting Insights Research

None of the methods described above is particularly difficult, but when people first start doing this kind of research, they are tempted to try them all at once. If you fall into this trap, you will get in a muddle and end up with a massive load of data that probably lacks focus.

Methods are tools and, like any other tool, sometimes it is the right one for the job and sometimes not. If you are not getting the kind of insights you need, try a different approach. Sometimes you might find that the "wrong" tool borrowed from another discipline works really well, rather like using a screwdriver to open a can of paint. You should be able to back up your research, but don't become a method fundamentalist. In the end, it is the results that you get and how rigorous and actionable they are that matter, not whether you used method A versus method B.

This kind of field research requires practice. If you have never done it before, you will make mistakes. There is a lot more to think about and a lot more multitasking required than most people who have never done it imagine. Try lining up less "important" interviews earlier on, such as people not really in your target group or friends who would not mind repeating the interview if necessary. This helps you practice your interview routine before you get to the CEO or the expert who only has a 30-minute time window for you.

Here are some more tips to help things run smoothly.

Be Prepared

Know what you want to find out, but don't be afraid of going a little off track if the subject goes in an interesting direction. Have some questions to ask, but not hundreds. Have areas and themes you want to cover and use these to direct the conversation. An interview should not be an interrogation, but it can quickly turn into one if you are nervous. The solution for being nervous? Be prepared.

Getting There

Make sure you know exactly where you are going. Get a map of the local area (or get your smartphone loaded up with a map or navigation app). Have a contact number for the person you are visiting and have your phone fully charged and in silent mode. Make sure you are on time. If you are going to be late, let the interviewee know. Meet the cultural expectations for punctuality. For example, in Britain and the United States, arriving too early can be worse than arriving late. In Germany and Switzerland, five minutes early is considered almost too late.

Identify Yourself

Introduce yourself when you arrive, and give the participant your business card as proof that you are who you say you are. If you are a student, take a letter from your institution signed by your lecturer. Business cards are so cheap to digitally print these days, however, it is worth having some printed up with your name and contact details. The participant should also be given your contact details because he or she may have the right to withdraw information at any time. Before you start the interview, briefly describe your organization, the general subject and purpose of the interview, and what you will be doing with the data you collect.

Taking Pictures

The process of photography can spark new conversations that might not have happened just by asking questions. Taking panoramas of rooms can help record many things you might miss in single shots. It can be helpful to ask participants to point out interesting things you should photograph. The things they see as important or valued can provide insights in themselves.

The kind of camera you use can be important. If it is too big and professional looking, it can be intimidating for participants. A combination of small but high-quality digital cameras and mobile phone cameras are usually fine (smartphone cameras can be high quality, but often fail in poor lighting). It is important to tell people why you are taking photos and how they will be used. If participants prefer that you not photograph something, don't push them. Tell them you understand, but try to keep a mental image instead and then write it down immediately after the visit while it is still fresh in your mind.

Materials

Bringing materials with you for users to fill in or discuss can really help get the conversation going. If you give participants a simple paper task, it can work not only as a record for you to keep and refer to but also as an icebreaker. As participants engage in the task, they might ask questions that lead to new and interesting topics.

Keep the materials fairly low key. Sketches of a website can lead to much more open comments than having perfect printouts of mockup screens, for example. When people see a mock-up printout, they will often assume the design is set in stone, whereas a sketch is obviously a work in progress and elicits more constructive criticism.

When making materials for people to use after a visit, such as a probe camera or a diary, it is again important to get the right balance between professional and handmade. If something is too perfect, participants will not want to spoil it. If it is too generic (such as a store-bought blank note-book), they may ignore it.

Dress Appropriately

"Dressing down" can be even more important than "dressing up." When visiting people in their homes, you probably do not want to wear a suit. This level of formality can keep people from feeling at ease and affect the way they respond to your questions. Likewise, scruffy jeans and T-shirts don't work well when interviewing bank managers at their workplace.

We find that the office-casual approach works well for home visits, and we keep our suits and ties for the formal visits. At the risk of sounding like your mother, home visits also require decent socks! You may be asked to remove your shoes when entering someone's home, and holes in your socks are not a good start to an interview.

If you are shadowing someone in their job, it is best to dress as they would (Figure 4.16). If you are researching within an organization that has some kind of uniform, it might be appropriate to wear the uniform. Whether you can do this or not is a decision that must be made by the organization you are working with, but can really help the other uniformed workers relate to you. It shows that you have made an effort to literally step into their shoes. Remember, though, that you are now representing your client's company, especially if you are in a customer-facing environment, so take it seriously.

A customer will not know that you are not a member of the staff and may ask you for help. If it is something more than asking directions to the restroom, you may want to explain that you are just there to do some research and politely point them in the direction of a real staff member.

FIGURE 4.16
Ben dressed in scrubs for some insights research at a hospital. A participating researcher needs to wear the right clothes to fit in.

Release Forms

Make sure the participant has signed the release form that you have prepared in advance. Typically, you should do this at the start of the interview, but it pays to double-check at the end; and in some spontaneous interview research (such as at an event where you want to capture immediate reactions), you might only be able to do it afterward. The release is a contract between your agency and the participant stating that the participant has given consent for his or her opinions to be used. It should also state how you intend to use the interview material and the level of confidentiality. You should take two copies of this document to the interview, one for the participant to keep and one to retain for your records.

Incentives

Depending on the subject of the research, incentives might be appropriate. For some projects, such as those involving health issues or the local community, people may be willing to help for free. For other, more commercial projects, an incentive can help ensure that participants feel committed to taking the interview seriously. The incentive might be cash, a voucher, or other benefit. Make sure you get participants to sign something to say they have received their incentive (this can be part of the release form).

Thank People

It is important to properly thank people at the end of the visit and to convey just how valuable their contribution is to the project. Many people will wonder why you are so interested in their lives. They may think they have been telling you banal facts, so telling them just how interesting and useful their input has been will end the session on a good note.

Collating and Presenting Your Insights

In Chapter 5, we look at mapping out a service ecology and the process of service design blueprinting in detail, which is how we start to visualize and understand the complexity of a service and make sense of our data. The insights we have gathered flow into this process, but first we need to synthesize the data that we have collected into a form that can be presented and discussed.[8]

The different forms we can use are relatively standard in design. They range from sticky notes, whiteboard sketches, and printouts on the wall to digital tools and more formal presentation forms. Below are three approaches to working with the results of insights research that we find useful.

Insights Blogs

A blog is essential for larger insights research projects and for when a client needs insights feedback quickly. It provides a complete record of interviews or other insights research that can easily be accessed and digested by the client. A blog allows the project to be shared with the entire company, promoting longevity (Figure 4.17). Blogs also prove useful as archives and can usually be exported in a number of common formats if they need to be taken offline.

Blogs can be set up quickly on intranet or extranet servers, and are easily updated by multiple researchers. This is especially useful on projects with nationwide or international scope, with researchers collecting data independently from remote locations. You can even set up a template so they have a standard form to use for writing and uploading their data, which helps bring some conformity to the qualitative data and makes it easier to compare.

---

8   An excellent treatise on the subject is Jon Kolko's *Exposing the Magic of Design: A Practitioner's Guide to the Methods and Theory of Synthesis* (New York: Oxford University Press, 2011).

FIGURE 4.17
An insights blog is a useful way to collate, present, and share data.

Insights Boards

Insights boards can be used to present insights based on real people who have been interviewed as an alternative to using fabricated personas. It is important to include photographs on each board to help people relate to the participant.

The boards should be able to be read at three levels: a headline quote, a series of key insights (backed up with quotes), and a larger paragraph of narrative text (Figure 4.18). Boards are often used to present insights in a client workshop as a way to get people thinking about improvements and innovations. Incidentally, insights blogs often use a similar format, with headline quote, key insights, and text, but more detail can be included in the blog entries than will fit onto a physical board. On the other hand, physical boards are more useful in a workshop than a digital version on a projector, which can only display one image at a time. Boards can all remain on display for inspiration and reference.

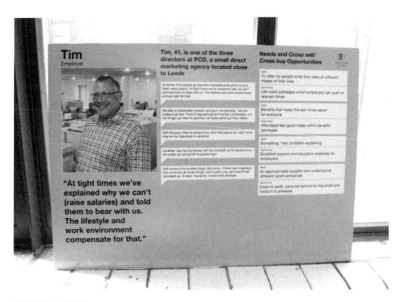

FIGURE 4.18
Insights can be printed on large boards for presentation of the research insights or for inspiration in a workshop setting.

Client Workshops

Presenting insights in a workshop environment is a good way to help clients understand the results. Together you can discover needs and opportunities and use these insights as inspiration to help generate ideas, usually in the form of sketches. This shows the value of this kind of research to the client and involves them in the design process early on, which should make it easier to explain your design solutions later on in the project.

The ideal client workshop size is 6 to 12 people. Bigger numbers do not necessarily mean better ideas and can sometimes degenerate into factions or leave certain participants isolated. On the other hand, a project might require bringing different groups of people together, which will mean your workshop might be bigger than this. In that case you will need to mix the groups to avoid factions and also have more moderators and helpers there to guide the individual groups (Figure 4.19). In some cases, you might have clients and customers in a mixed workshop to explore how to improve services or to test out some new propositions or prototypes.

FIGURE 4.19
Client workshops help people discover needs, opportunities, and new ideas. This is a large workshop with moderated mixed groups of different stakeholders.

Our advice for preparing user workshops also goes for preparing client workshops. It may not always be possible, but try to find a venue outside of the client's offices. People are often able to think more creatively when they are not in their usual work environment. Be well prepared! The stakes are somewhat higher with client workshops, because you are on display, but this means you also have an opportunity to show clients what you do and get them involved—something that many designers in other disciplines never get the chance to do.

Summary

If service design is about people and relationships, then we need to find out what makes people tick. Insights research methods in service design draw heavily on those from ethnography, sociology, and human-centered design. There are others, however, that are service-design specific. The level of detail that you can go into will depend on your budget, but the three levels of low (what they say), middle (what we saw), and high (what it means) is a good way to orient your work. You will need to present your research and insights clearly to either the rest of the design team or to your clients. This kind of research can involve a steep learning curve if you have never done it before, but is usually extremely engaging. The key is to be prepared.

Insights Research Checklist

Things to take with you:

- Notebook and pens

- Camera or camera phone

- Dictaphone or video camera

- Release form/receipt

- Business card, as proof of identity

- Incentive payment

- Interview topic guide

Things to remember:

- Do you have a list of the key topics you want to cover?

- Are your phone and camera fully charged?

- Do you know exactly where you are going?

- Have you worked out how you will get there and back?

- Do you have a contact number for the person you are meeting? Do they know you are coming?

- Does someone else know where you are going?

- Are you dressed appropriately?

Summary continues on next page

Summary (continued)

These questions will help you a get a feel for the participant's background and help you think outside of your topic when you want to get a sense of the person's general motivations and opinions:

- Tell me about your family.
- Tell me about your job.
- What did you do last weekend?
- What did you do yesterday?
- What did you have for dinner last night?
- Who did you talk with yesterday?

CHAPTER 5

Describing the Service Ecology

As you start gathering insights and other background material for a project, you will need to structure this information in some way. In this chapter we discuss the role of the service blueprint, which helps you structure, design, and align touchpoint interactions as they unfold over time. First, though, it is sometimes necessary to gain a sense of the context in which the service is operating, which is usually complex. You can map this out in a service ecology—a diagram of all the actors affected by a service and the relationships between them, displayed in a systematic manner.

A service ecology can start off simple—for instance, as a map that shows how a customer might use a website in combination with a call center to solve a problem. At the other end of the scale, it is possible to map complex systems such as a public transportation system or a model for reducing unemployment.

The basic actors in a service ecology are the *enterprises* that make a promise to the customer (or service user), the *agents* who deliver that promise through different channels, and the *customers* who return value back to the enterprise (Figure 5.1).

From a branding point of view, the enterprise makes a promise to the service user and expects value in return, whether by payment, tax, or labor. For example, a mobile provider gives its customers airtime and data in return for payment. A city provides street lighting and clears away trash in return for taxes. An employee receives a salary in return for his or her labor. As a side note here, when we talk about "enterprise" and "branding," this may be in either a commercial or a nonprofit/public service context.

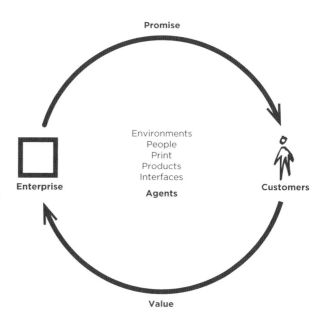

FIGURE 5.1
A basic customer–enterprise service ecology. The enterprise makes a promise to its customers, which is delivered by its agents through different channels. The customers return value, usually in the form of money.

The enterprise itself does not deliver experiences and utility to people, however. These are provided by the agents who are in direct contact with users through channels and touchpoints. Channels are the overall medium, such as e-mail, telephone, and face-to-face, and a touchpoint is an individual moment of interaction within that channel, such as a single call or an e-mail exchange. So, a customer might interact with several touchpoints across a single channel or across many channels. The role of the enterprise is to deliver the tools and infrastructure that agents need to deliver a good service experience.

The point of using the metaphor of ecologies when describing services is not only that services often harbor a complexity that can be compared to systems in nature. Looking at services as ecologies also emphasizes the point that *all* of the actors in a service exchange some sort of value. When customers pay a bill online, they save the bank money and they enjoy the convenience of banking outside regular banking hours. When users navigate a simple Web page, they leave behind data that enable the provider to improve the site, and the users do not have to fill in a load of details again when they return. A healthy ecology is one in which everyone benefits, rather than having the value flow in one direction only.

The most common lost opportunity is when enterprises neglect the resource that customers can be in terms of providing value back to the service. Customers are usually motivated to provide labor, knowledge, and data if these will help them get a better result, and when customers invest in the outcome, they connect more strongly to the brand.

Enterprises can do far more to help customers return value to both themselves and other service users. In general, the relationship between service users and the enterprise is very one-sided. Taxpayers who submit their tax returns after the deadline can be fined, but the tax office may take months to complete their side of the deal with no penalty. If travelers turn up five minutes late to check in with a budget airline, they can expect to miss the flight or pay a hefty surcharge (and often receive less-than-charming responses from staff). Yet when a flight is late and travelers miss their connection, it is their own hard luck.

Failing to provide resources in the form of communication channels for this return of value from the service user to the enterprise is dangerous. The Internet has given people the ability to easily create their own forums to voice their views and experiences, completely outside of the enterprise and often negative in tone. During the period we have been writing this book, we have seen the rise of the Arab Spring and the Occupy Wall Street movements, for example, which are powerful examples of self-organized value communication channels. Organizations can panic and view these voices as a loss of command and control, or they can view them as valuable feedback and make use of it. After all, the main purpose of paying someone to do insights research is to find out about these views, beliefs, and motivations. It makes sense to build it into the service ecology from the start.

A more detailed model of the service relationship includes much more exchange (Figure 5.2). The promise to the customer is fulfilled when agents provide utility and experience to customers through activities across the various channels, known as "frontstage" in service design (see "The Service Blueprint" below). Customers return added value to the enterprise through cooperation, information, and feedback, along with payment for services.

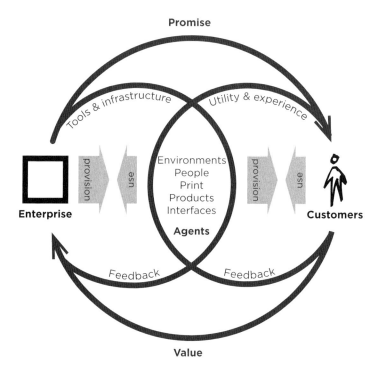

FIGURE 5.2
A detailed model of the service relationship. Frontstage, the promise to the customer is fulfilled when agents provide utility and experi- ence and customers return added value to the enterprise through cooperation, information, and feedback. Backstage, the agents need tools and infrastructure to deliver utility and a good experience to customers. These tools also provide feedback in the form of data, which can be used to monitor and improve the service.

On the enterprise side, agents need tools and infrastructure "backstage" to deliver the utility and experience to the customer. These tools also provide feedback in the form of data, which can be used to monitor and improve the service. All of these flows need to be designed to deliver a good service.

The final point about the service ecology metaphor is that just like in nature, the actors in a service constantly change and evolve. In fact, services like Amazon and eBay make frequent small changes to their interfaces based on customer data, and a service delivered by a human changes with every employee. This means services need to be designed with enough resilience to handle constant changes in the machinery. One of the reasons co-design and client involvement is so important throughout the process is because staff need to learn the tools so they can make minor adjustments without having to call in the service designers every time. Management need to give staff the responsibility and flexibility to make changes in response to their environment.

Why Map Service Ecologies?

The example in Figure 5.2 is very simple, but services can be very complex once you take in the context and all of the actors involved. Designing an entire ecosystem is impossible, so service ecology maps are particularly useful in the early phases of design projects. They give you a means to establish a shared overview of the space you wish to work within.

The service ecology map has three main purposes:

1.   To map service actors and stakeholders

2.   To investigate relationships that are part of or affect the service

3.   To generate new service concepts by reorganizing how actors work together

As an exercise, mapping a service ecology can be very effective in a client workshop as a means to broaden the project space. It helps people to think beyond their own business or organizational concerns and see how what they are doing fits into the wider context of people's lives and society. At the same time, it is important not to fall in love with the mapping exercise itself. Service ecologies can grow infinitely large, and if you do not focus on the results you are looking for, you can end up having mapped the whole world and not know what to do with it. It is important to define the boundaries of the map so you do not continue on forever. Some of this scope is defined by the project's strategic goals, budget, sphere of influence, and so on, but the boundaries will also become clearer as you do the mapping exercise.

Figure 5.3 maps the ecology of a potential car-sharing service for FIAT and deals with the scope of the project by visualizing a series of levels that enabled the design team to focus in and out on the essential relationships of the service. The center describes the relationship between the driver and the car, and then expands to passengers, other cars, other services, communities, and at the perimeter, the Earth. (See how easily you can end up there?)

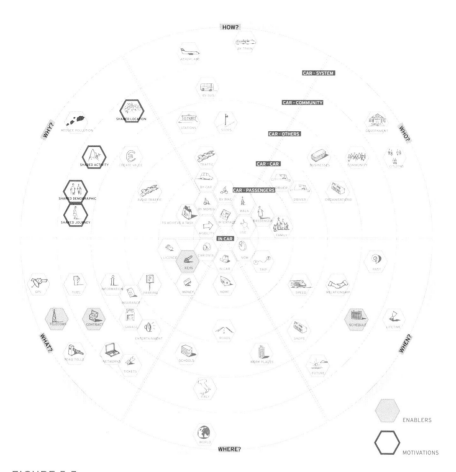

FIGURE 5.3

A map of actors involved in or affected by a new car-sharing scheme. This map was created for FIAT's Future Design Group as part of a project at Interaction Design Institute Ivrea in Italy.

The map was designed using icons printed onto honeycomb-shaped cards that enabled the project participants to combine actors in different ways to produce service concepts. As an example, connecting a community to a car revealed the potential of a business model in which FIAT could get a town to pay for a shared car to provide more flexible transportation for its citizens. The hexagonal shape of the cards allowed more elements to connect with each other than is possible with standard rectangular cards, but a set of sticky notes on a whiteboard suffices most of the time.

Ultimately, the project led to design proposals ranging from a redesign of the car key enable multiple users to share a car, to a concept for integrating the car's computer with public transportation information so that car club members could hop in a passing car rather than wait for the bus (Figure 5.4).

FIGURE 5.4
A concept image for connecting shared cars with public transportation information.

The development of the service ecology map helped make connections between different services that would normally have been overlooked. And making some quick mock-ups of the concepts at this early stage helps people imagine what the service might look like in reality. It also helps people to start thinking about the details, such as the privacy issues raised by the system shown in Figure 5.4, or just what it might mean for many people to have keys to the same car. Making the experience and proposition tangible helps highlight these details. We discuss this in more detail in the experience prototyping section in Chapter 7.

The Network Society

Around 1970, when the authors of this book were born, the developed world was well on its way to shifting from industrial societies to networked societies. Since then, organizations have steadily broken down strict hierarchies and favored models in which units are smaller, more independent, and collaborative. At the same time, network technology has developed at accelerating speed. These two social and technological trends are not necessarily driven by the same causes, but they have powered each other to form radically new platforms of service delivery. [1]

The maturation of these platforms has served as the foundation for the emergence of service design as a coherent design discipline over the past 10 to 15

---

1 See the work of Manuel Castells for a detailed account of these social changes; for example, *The Rise of the Network Society*, vol. 1, *The Information Age: Economy, Society and Culture*, 2nd ed. (Malden, MA: Blackwell, 2000).

years. It is a discipline fundamentally driven by networks. It is why designers have come to work on complex transportation, banking, and healthcare systems, not simply customer services or individual products or touchpoints.

These systems present a different type of complexity than industrial products. Products require designers to deal with many moving parts, but services require us to design systems that adapt well to constantly changing parts. Networks, organizations, and technology evolve on a daily basis, but the service still needs to deliver a robust customer experience.

Whether you need a way to approach "multichannel experiences," "Web 2.0," or some other current trend, service design offers tools and models that enable you to design for complexity.

There is no shortage of disciplines engaged in the design of touchpoints. Graphic design, UX design, product design, interaction design, information architecture, and customer experience design are just a few in a long list. These fields are still essential and used in the process of delivering service touchpoints. But this fact begs the question, "Why are so many service experiences awful when parts of them are seemingly well designed?"

Boxes versus Arrows— Finding the Invisible Connections

The answer to why so many services are poorly designed lies in the lack of attention paid to the invisible elements of time and context, both of which are critical to the experience of a service.

Arrows and lines in organizational charts and process diagrams often represent time, context, and connections. The problem is that arrows and connecting lines are so ubiquitous in diagrams that they are ignored. It is much easier to focus design effort on the boxes because they represent tangible touchpoints—the website, the ticket machine, and so on—but most people forget to think about designing the experience of the arrows, which are the transitions from one touchpoint to the next. Yet these connections contain some of the most important elements of positive experiences because they signify movement in time and space. It is as if companies spend fortunes building gleaming towers and cities while the roads between them are muddy dirt tracks. But people spend a lot of time traveling those tracks.

Silos within organizations can prevent engaging and positive service experiences from happening, because the seemingly small cracks between the individual silo elements, such as the discrepancies between online and in-store offerings, can soon open up into experience crevasses.

This is especially true of services because they usually unfold over time. Unlike a product, which customers purchase once and may use over time, services are usually the process of a time-based experience. A hotel stay is made up of many different experiences across a number of channels, from a Web search to find a place to stay, to booking, to the chocolate on the pillow, to the checkout procedure. Air travel, or even just buying the ticket, is something that happens over time. Long-term services, such as healthcare, finance, and insurance, affect people throughout their lifetimes.

All experiences of a service are a result of interactions of some kind. Obvious interactions are various touchpoints such as objects, interfaces, and interpersonal interactions. Less obvious are interactions between previous experiences or beliefs. Think of people's fear of the dentist due to childhood experiences, an entire country being written off as a tourist destination because of one bad meal in a dodgy hotel, or the complexity of human emotions displayed by patients, carers, and medical workers in a healthcare service.

Service experiences are also affected by the contexts of time and place, and the most amazing thing at the wrong time can be more of a service design failure than something average that is delivered at exactly the right moment. Think of a romantic dinner interrupted by the restaurant violinist blaring away while a couple is trying to have a quiet conversation, or a helpful nurse arriving with a delicious meal just after a loved one has died. Some of the best service experiences are like the ideal wine waiter—there when he is needed, but somehow invisible when he is not.

A critical aspect of designing services is understanding context, and this is where service design is different from what many designers understand as user-centered design approaches. Our experience of UX design and interaction design is that the processes tend to be focused on individual touchpoints, and those touchpoints are, more often than not, digital and on-screen. This is in no way a criticism of these disciplines—we all have experience in them and use their processes and methods as part of the service design palette. It is more an observation of the areas that UX design and interaction design commonly engage in.

As we mentioned in Chapter 2, services are often created in silos and experienced in bits. Getting some companies to move from management silos, in which the customer may not ever feature, to a customer-centered perspective is already a massive improvement. Such companies may even use a diagram that looks something like the one in Figure 2.3.

With this in mind, different disciplines and departments can feel comfortable that they understand and are taking care of the customer experience. The Web and mobile team can look at their touchpoints, design them well, take a strong UX approach, and argue their case, but are the silos really dissolved? Taking another look at Figure 2.3, we see that if the connections (the arrows connecting the channels) are ignored, the silos are still potentially there, but they are just arranged in a circle.

It is difficult to recount bad service experience stories without immediately sounding like a grumpy old man. Nevertheless, this account of my (Lavrans) trying to book a flight for my family is a good example of how several small cracks in the experience of a service can lead to an experience crevasse.

Two months before flying from New York to Oslo with my family, I sit down to book the tickets for three adults, a four-year-old, and a six-month-old baby.

Website–Call Center Gap

The website does not allow me to book a seat for a child younger than one year. Maybe they are trying to force us to fly with the baby on our laps for free? In any case, I feel we need the extra seat to get across the ocean with our sanity intact, so I call customer support. No problem, I'm told, just book another seat for a one-year-old and ignore the fact that this does not match the passenger details.

Back in the website booking process, the assigned seats I get are distributed across the cabin. I'm not allowed to change the seating now, so I relax and plan to do it online when I'm invited to check in 24 hours before the flight.

Website–System Error Gap

Unfortunately, at online check-in I still can't change our seat assignments. In fact, as I attempt to do it, I lose the seats we had and I'm left with no seats to my name. At this point I'm starting to worry about us getting on the plane at all. I envision airport scenes where I am fighting with staff who will be fighting with computer systems, all with a crying baby on my arm and a furious wife at my side.

Website–Call Center Gap

Determined to get everything under control, I call customer service. The empathetic customer representative does his best to get our seats reassigned, but has to explain to me that he does not have any access rights to the system beyond what I have online and cannot assign my seats. He assures me that the check-in staff at the airport will take care of the problem and that they always make sure families are seated together. "Just make sure you get there early," he counsels. I am half convinced, but feel the need to prepare a backup plan. I look up information on other flights, places to stay overnight, and car rental services.

Husband–Wife Expectation Gap

At this point I feel I need to tell my wife about the potential problem. I am willing to pay the price for shared uncertainty in return for setting her expectations correctly so we can deal with the potential problems together. Anyone who has flown long haul with small children can identify with the fear of a 48-hour stay in an international airport terminal. Like all the other humans involved in the process, my wife is determined to do her best to deal with the situation.

Call Center Staff–Check-In Staff Gap

When we get to the airport the next day, my scepticism turns out to be justified. We arrive early as told, and the check-in staff cannot assign us seats before the plane is ready to board at the gate. Still seatless we settle in to wait, but at least we have tickets. They have checked our bags, so we are fairly certain that we will get on the plane. They even checked our extra bag for free.

Boarding Staff–Computer System Gap

After a couple of hours in the airport keeping on top of changing departure gates, I learn that our plane is parked and that boarding staff are at the gate. I run over, with the baby on my arm, to make sure I'm the first person to create problems for the fresh staff before they are overwhelmed.

The boarding staff treat me well and make it clear that they understand I feel my request is a priority because I am traveling with small children. Unfortunately, the two employees end up arguing over how to deal with the computer. One of them claims to know the best way to cheat the system and get us seated together.

They tell me to take a seat and that they will come over with our tickets when they are ready. The human service element finally wins, and a few minutes later we are handed our tickets with a smile—seated together.

A day of worry and preparation for the things that could go wrong came to a happy end. However, much energy was spent and a great deal of stress created to achieve the result I expected in the first place.

What Can We Learn from This Story?

- Gaps between silos that seem small from the provider's point of view accumulate to form experience crevasses for the customer. A service design approach that joins the silos together from a customer perspective can make a huge difference.

- Staff usually try to do their best, but the systems they work within often prevent them from doing so.

- Dealing with problems with a baby on your arm will make people treat you better, but this should not need to be the case.

The key to a seamless service experience is taking care to understand the contexts in which users interact with touchpoints and services. A good—or, rather, bad—example are the train ticket machines in Germany. After a recent upgrade, the graphic design of the screens is much more pleasant, but the overall interaction flow is slower and therefore worse due to the extra animation and display overhead. In the context of a design studio, the flow makes some sense, but in the context of rushing for a train and needing to buy a ticket, it is a disaster. The other context is the business of the machines themselves, usually designed and maintained by third-party organizations. Even when it is clear to the designers and researchers that the ticket machines are a problem, the company supplying and maintaining those machines usually resists changes, citing IT support issues. The only thing the design team is allowed to change are the graphics; they are not even allowed to touch the layout.

Many companies have an online (essentially mail-order) offering as well as bricks-and-mortar stores. They may offer special online deals that are not available in their stores, and some stores are official stores whereas others are simply franchises or resellers, which is often the case in telecommunications and insurance. The customer, however, experiences these—or expects to experience them—as a coherent brand and does not understand or is frustrated by the discrepancies. Why can't the store offer the online cell phone plan, for example? There are usually "good" business reasons why these differences exist—an online transaction is basically self-service and therefore cheaper for the company—but for the customer they are a series of small irritations that add up to a terrible overall experience of the service.

From Ecology Map to Service Blueprint

The service ecology map gives us the bird's-eye view of the ecosystem a service exists within, and the insights research gives us the bottom-up view from the stakeholders. As Lavrans's story illustrates (see sidebar on page 88), the real effort goes into aligning everything and mapping out the middle elements that will actually form the design work to create the seamless (we hope) service experience. If you turn the traditional management model of silos in Figure 2.1 by 90 degrees, you will see something interesting—the customer/user is at the top, the enterprise is at the bottom, and all of the channels of interaction are in between (Figure 5.5). This is the beginning of the service blueprint.

FIGURE 5.5
Turning the traditional silo model of an organization 90 degrees and looking at it from the point of view of the customer journey dramatically improves the opportunity to join up the bits and deliver a consistent customer experience.

The Service Blueprint

Connecting together all of the different touchpoints in a service experience, as well as aligning the needs and wishes of all of an organization's stakeholders, can become very complex very quickly, which is where service blueprinting comes in.

G. Lynn Shostack pioneered the idea of a service blueprint and coined the term in the early 1980s while she was a vice president of Citibank in the United States.[2] Shostack developed the service blueprint as a way to plan the cost and revenue associated with operating a service, and her early versions looked very much like flow diagrams (Figure 5.6).

The example in Figure 5.6 is a simple one of a shoeshine service, but it introduced two key elements: time in the form of the customer service experience, and the line of visibility, which is essentially everything that the customer sees. Actually, it is everything the customer *experiences* because bad smells or loud noises can just as easily sour a customer experience.

This line of visibility has since been augmented in other designers' models by lines of "external interaction" (all the things the "customer" interacts with) and "internal interaction" (all the things that service providers interact with).

2 G. Lynn Shostack, "How to Design a Service," *European Journal of Marketing* 16, no. 1 (1982): 49–63; and "Designing Services That Deliver," *Harvard Business Review* 62, no. 1 (1984): 133–39.

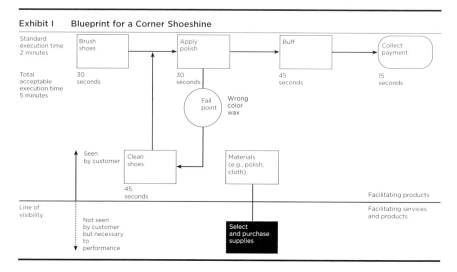

Exhibit I   Blueprint for a Corner Shoeshine

FIGURE 5.6
An early example of a service blueprint. From G. Lynn Shostack, "Designing Services That Deliver," *Harvard Business Review* 62, no. 1 (1984): 133–39.

Shostack's line of visibility has transmuted into the frontstage/backstage metaphor in which anything that the "customer" experiences is frontstage (on-stage would be more appropriate to the metaphor) and everything else that goes on behind the scenes to make that happen is backstage.

Orchestral or theatrical metaphors are now common in service design. Service designers may like the idea of comparing themselves to conductors or directors for obvious and egocentric reasons that are probably not very productive. However, the service as an orchestral or theatrical production is a valuable metaphor and an alternative to the traditional role of designers. Service is more performance than manufacture.

For example, the idea of a "set," or the setting of a service, is important because it enables us to think about the context in which staff and users interact. It also reminds us that things must work well backstage for the performance to be successful.

In classic theater, the actors have clearly defined roles, and from the beginning their goals are clear. What adds drama is how the actors face obstacles and overcome hurdles. Both staff and customers have specific things they wish to achieve, as in the classic dramaturgy of roles, motivations, and goals. The experience is defined by how they help each other reach a happy ending.

Finally, theater has props, which in service design terms are the touchpoints. These are the physical elements people use during the narrative, and they are crucial to enabling the drama to take place.

A classic example is a hotel stay—guests do not often see the activities of the staff who clean and make up the rooms (backstage), just the results (frontstage). Often, this backstage activity is evidenced in some way by bringing it frontstage, such as the folded toilet paper tip in a hotel bathroom that indicates the room has been cleaned.

The theatrical metaphor does have its limitations. Real people cannot be scripted, and we all know that the unexpected is bound to happen when people deliver or use a service. Services do not have fixed times when they start and finish, users often fail to "read their lines," and service providers are rarely in full control of their environments.

The most rewarding way to use the theatrical metaphor is to think about service as improvisational theater. If you provide users and staff with a good "stage" on which to interact, and give them well-defined roles, clear goals, and the necessary props, people are likely to make the most out of the situation and create great experiences together.

The stage metaphor can be a useful way of aligning organizational activities with the "customer" experience, but the reason why we have put *customer* in quotes is because services do not always follow a simple customer and service-provider construct. Another way to approach blueprints is to treat each person, or even each nonhuman actor (usually a computer), as a *role* and map out the interactions between them across the full range of touchpoints.

Over the years, service designers have developed the blueprint as a comprehensive tool for placing the customer and service stakeholders at the heart of service design and innovation projects. As service designers engage more deeply with their clients' processes and help them sort out their delivery systems, service design becomes central to clients' businesses and operations.

A service blueprint is a map of:

- The user journey—phase by phase, step by step
- The touchpoints—channel by channel, touchpoint by touchpoint
- The backstage processes—stakeholder by stakeholder, action by action

A typical service blueprint template might look like the one in Figure 5.7.

The good news is that a service blueprint is an extremely useful tool. Blueprints help to capture the big picture and interconnections, and are a way to plan out projects and relate service design decisions back to the original research insights. The blueprint is different from the service ecology in that it includes specific detail about the elements, experiences, and delivery within the service itself, whereas the service ecology diagrams the service at a much higher level and shows the entire service's relationship to other services and the surrounding environment in which it operates.

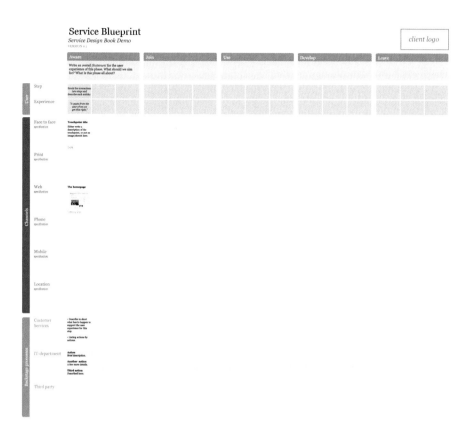

FIGURE 5.7

A typical service blueprint template, with the phases of the customer journey along the top (here it's Aware, Join, Use, Develop, Leave) and the various touchpoint channels in rows underneath, including the backstage activities at the bottom. A couple of touchpoints have been filled in as examples.

The bad news is that, unlike blueprints for engineering or architecture, there is no typical or "standard" service blueprint with commonly agreed terminology and visual language. Andy worked on a research project at the Hochschule Luzern that examined a range of blueprints, and the group found as many different flavors of the diagrams as there were organizations creating them.[3] Even within a single company, blueprints change in terms of design and content, sometimes requiring additional channels or more or fewer phases depending on the project and its purpose (Figure 5.8).

---

3 Andy Polaine, "Blueprint+: Developing a Tool for Service Design," Service Design Network conference, October 27, 2009, Madeira, www.slideshare.net/apolaine/blueprint-developing-a-tool-for-service-design.

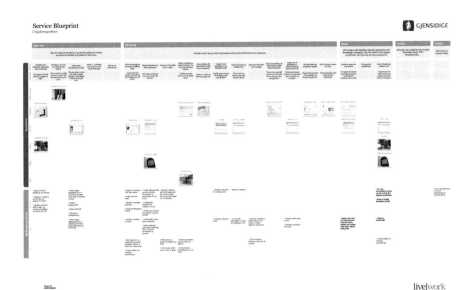

FIGURE 5.8
An example of a service blueprint with many touchpoints filled in.
The second phase has been extended to accommodate a number
of more detailed steps.

The underlying principles, however, remain the same. Essentially, you are
trying to map out the service ecology by tracking all the people involved in
its usage and delivery across all the relevant channels of communication
and interaction. And you are mapping out all of this as it unfolds over time
and connecting it to the insights research.

Engaging with real people provides insight on all levels of a service proposition. Do people value the service and the brand? Are they irritated by
details on the invoice? The challenge from a service perspective is to include
insights across the system in one picture.

The project team must then align insights from backstage staff with
customer needs and define *where* in the customer journey the experience
breaks down or great opportunities exist. Where do channels and technologies play well together to produce value, and when do they run counter to
each other? Finally, you will design or write the design specification for all of
the touchpoints.

Different Uses of Blueprints

The service blueprint offers a framework to categorize and work systematically with insight in complex networks. This puts you in the position of making concrete arguments about the design of the service, ranging from how to restructure the proposition to fixing a single crucial detail in the system. It also lays the groundwork for generating ideas and designing solutions that work across the network of people, technologies, and processes. As such, blueprinting is both a process of analysis and a method for generating ideas. These two overlap, of course. You might analyze an existing service, find problems, and then generate new innovations, all of which requires multiple iterations of the blueprint.

Blueprints and storyboard sketches (more detailed explanations of touch-points) are to service design what 3D sketches and wireframes are to product design and UX design. Just like an exploded view of an electric motor, a service blueprint provides an overview for everyone involved in the design and delivery to see how the bits of the service work as a whole. A blueprint helps to break down barriers between business units, and it reveals opportunities for joining up processes to create more seamless experiences.

Blueprints for Analysis of an Existing Service

In the past, when trying to test the quality of a service, we could not find one single method to measure quality in the way people experience it across touchpoints. The service blueprint maps how the service is constructed, connecting all the channels and touchpoints to the customer journey and the backstage processes that are required to deliver them. It gives service designers a platform to systematically test people's different journeys through the system. You can track their path across time and touchpoints, and reveal where real value was created and where opportunities were wasted. This tells you not only what is wrong, but also how to fix it.

Sometimes a failure behind the scenes that happens early in a process may not come to the surface until much later in the customer experience. For example, a poorly designed piece of communication, especially from a back-stage process such as billing, can lead to customer confusion and a high volume of calls to customer services.

This kind of blueprint-as-analysis is a useful tool to show clients the results of insights research and to highlight key areas where resources should be concentrated. In the Gjensidige project, for example, the design team discovered between 50 and 100 touchpoints that connected to the customer experience, depending on the customer's situation. Feeding touchpoint insights into a blueprint gives us a basis from which to work so that we can improve a service. It also gives us an overview that helps us decide which touchpoints to focus on during prototyping. Ideally, we want to work on the touchpoints that have the greatest impact on the service experience, but we do not know how they will work or feel until we see people interacting with them (see Chapter 7 for more on prototyping).

Blueprints for Service Innovation

The other use of a blueprint is when innovating new services, either as a strategic shift in an existing organization or because a market opportunity for a completely new business has been spotted. It is easy to get excited about a new and innovative service idea when it seems simple and compelling in your head, but it is equally easy for your imagination to end up working in silos. You might envisage a wonderful retail experience, for example, but forget to think about all the backstage things that need to happen for that experience to be a success.

Mapping out all of the stages in a blueprint helps you develop a much more coherent proposition because you can see how all the elements interlink and work over time. The other advantage of this step, creatively, is that the act of sketching out the blueprint usually gives rise to other ideas and connections you would not have thought of otherwise, which can help you develop new business propositions.

Although we describe a fairly comprehensive blueprinting process below, a quick thumbnail sketch of a blueprint grid, or even a four- or five-panel storyboard of the service usage experience, can really help you think through a service concept in the early ideation stages. Because services are complex, you may miss a critical point of failure when thinking through a service concept. You may also have difficulty communicating your concept to others without showing how some key elements of the service unfold over time. Sometimes a quick storyboard sketch helps you realize that an idea is a nonstarter, and learning this after a couple of hours of work is better than after a few months of effort.

Most projects involve a combination of the two blueprinting approaches. Some improvement work may be the initial foot in the door that leads to new service innovation projects later. Sometimes a radical, blue-sky innovation session leads to smaller improvements in an existing service.

Start with Broad Phases and Activities

Whether you are working on improvement, new service innovation, or a mixture of both, the first step in creating a blueprint is to establish the stages of the service experience over time—the service life cycle—and then add the roles of the people involved in the service (usually starting with the customer or service user) and the touchpoint channels. These can be laid out in a grid consisting of the various roles and channels down the side and the time phases across the top (Figure 5.9).

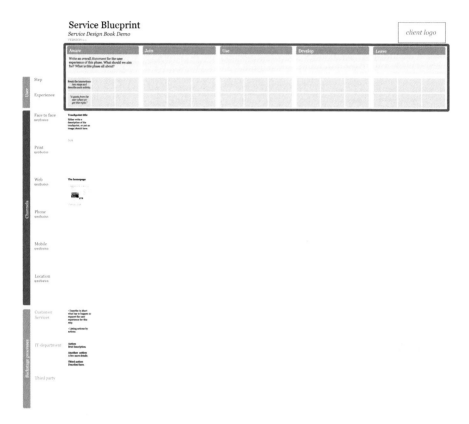

FIGURE 5.9

The blueprint is a grid with the phases and steps of time running along the horizontal axis, and the customer, touchpoint channels, and other stakeholders along the vertical axis.

As we mentioned, there are no standard or typical blueprints and each project or element of a project may require different phases, but it usually makes sense to start with a default set of broader user journey phases across the top of the grid (Figure 5.10). The ones we typically use are listed below.

- **Aware:** The point when the user first learns about the service
- **Join:** The sign-up or registration phase
- **Use:** The usual usage period of the service
- **Develop:** The user's expanding usage of the service
- **Leave:** The point when the user finishes using the service, either for a single session or forever

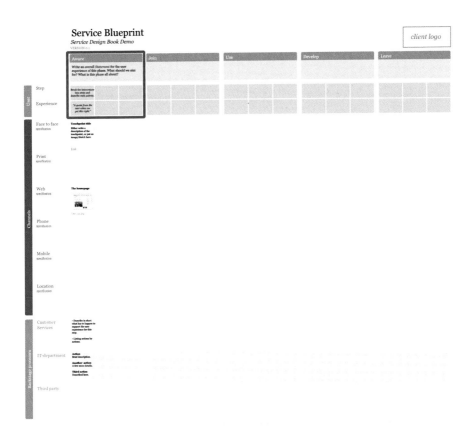

FIGURE 5.10

Start the blueprinting process by mapping out the main phases across the top of the grid. Each phase should be fairly broad, such as "Aware" or "Use."

You will want to come up with phases specific to your project, such as "check in" or "close account," and you may want to break down some phases into more detailed steps, especially for the "Use" and "Develop" phases (Figure 5.11). Add a brief description of the phase or step if it helps create clarity. This descriptive text is especially useful in blueprints that focus only on the substeps within a certain phase.

Use whatever level of granularity you need for your project, but be careful not to mix up the levels of detail too much. Detailed, step-by-step screens of a Web service sign-up process, for example, really belong in the set of wireframe documents that will specify this touchpoint later. Too much detail in a service blueprint can reduce its ability to provide a useful overview.

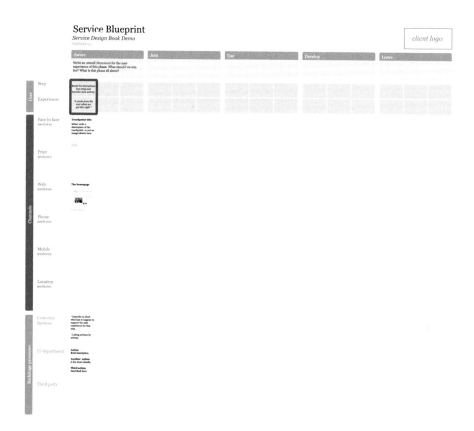

FIGURE 5.11

Break down the main phases—Aware, Join, Use, Develop, Leave—into smaller substeps if needed. For example, an airline arrivals hall Use phase might include steps such as "Arrive," "Find check-in counter," "Check bags," "Receive boarding pass," and "Go through security." Each of these is represented as a thinner column that spans all the touchpoints at that step.

Add the Touchpoint Channels

Notice that the broad phases listed above are described in terms of types of activity, such as "join" or "use." These do not address the question of *how* these phases are carried out, such as "Sign up via the website form." This step comes next when you add the various touchpoint channels to the left-hand side of the blueprint. Each row of the blueprint represents a channel of touchpoints (Figure 5.12).

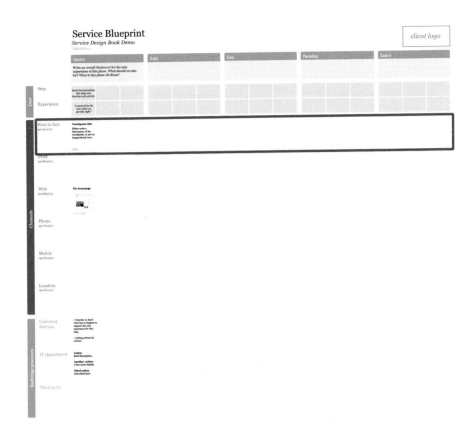

FIGURE 5.12

Each row below the customer journey phases represents a channel of touchpoints, such as "Print," "Face to face," "Web," and "Phone."

These channels will almost certainly include media channels such as print, e-mail, and a website, but they may also include people in the form of staff or other stakeholders. The service may also include interaction with products, third-party services, and even other customers or users. The list of channels can extend down as far as you need. The number of rows is determined by the project context, but sometimes having a larger set of touchpoints than you initially imagine can help broaden the scope of your "What if?" thinking. [4] If your project lends itself to division into frontstage and backstage activities, as most will, you can also do this here.

---

4   Simon Clatworthy from the Oslo School of Architecture has developed a set of cards, each with a different type of touchpoint printed on it. They are useful for reminding yourself of the many possible touchpoints in a service, and you can even use the cards to stimulate brainstorming activities for services. They are available for free if you contact him through his website. Details are on the "Touch-point Cards Now Available" page at www.service-innovation.org/?p=577.

Even simple services have many touchpoints, and comprehensive services can become very complex to map out. If you add other people interacting in roles, such as patient, nurse, doctor, and administrative staff, you will find the blueprint becomes very complex very quickly. The idea is to capture the overall picture of the service concept as well as the specific details that make up the touchpoint experiences. Blueprints offer a way to manage the complexity. It is also important to be able to think through the journeys between the various touchpoints. For example, it is no good if the patient's experience with the doctor and in the CT scanning room are wonderful if the patient has to wait for hours in a dimly lit hospital hallway while sitting on uncomfortable furniture.

Now that you have your grid, you can start filling in each cell representing the individual touchpoint experiences (Figure 5.13).

If you are analyzing an existing service, you can start by adding the results of your insights research. Write a statement in each cell to describe the experience of each moment of interaction—the customer trying to sign up online for a new mobile phone contract, for example, or interactions with staff in a store. At the "zoomed-out" blueprint level, these should be just a few words and some simple sketches. If you have space, you might want to add a photo or sketch that may describe things better than you can with words.

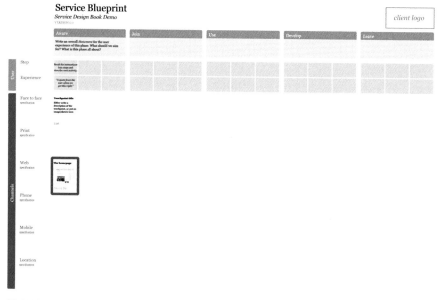

FIGURE 5.13
Each cell represents a single touchpoint experience in a single phase or step of the journey.

If you are developing a new service, think through how all the touch-points connect together as a complete experience. This is also true if you are improving an existing service, but in this case you will have to decide whether this iteration of your blueprint is intended as an analytical tool to uncover problems or whether you want to include all the new ideas in it, too.

The Journey from Products to Services

by Chris Risdon

Just a few years ago, I thought of myself as a designer of digital products—an interaction designer in the field of user experience focused on making digital products usable, engaging, and yes, profitable. But a funny thing has happened over the past few years: the projects I worked on started to look a lot less like products and more like services.

I went from designing something that was used in a single context (say, sitting at a computer looking at a browser) and roughly the same way with each use, to something that was used in different contexts and potentially used differently in each of those instances. Instead of designing a digital thing, I was designing to support a less tangible, ongoing sequence of interactions over time, between a customer and a company.

And it wasn't just digital. Increasingly, the work I was doing for a product system was finding its way to other parts of an organization and its service offering. Their call center and their retail or environmental experience were all able to benefit from the insights we gained from research gathered for the digital product channel. It became hard to conduct research and gain insights for the digital channel without it having explicit influence on other channels or areas of a company's offering. Customers don't think in channels, and they don't recognize that they are switching channels, so we couldn't simply confine ourselves to designing for a single channel and think the customer would have a consistent, satisfying experience. We may have thought we were designing digital products, but customers were having interactions with the company that manifested in both tangible and intangible ways.

With this new focus on product systems, I needed new methods to capture this experience—methods that captured a system, not a single product, and that illustrated the way this system was used over time and in those changing contexts. I also needed something that would bring together the different parts of the organization. Clearly, user experience principles can be applied much more widely than to digital channels, but it is still primarily a practice for designing discreet digital products, its methods are not necessarily designed to go broad—cross-channel and cross-organization. Terms, methods, and processes may conflate in the future, but service design activities are more inherently suited, currently, to cross silos and incorporate other channels. It is explicitly less about the discrete in absence of the whole. Both disciplines seek to take a customer-centered approach to designing a product or service, so there's no reason why they shouldn't be complementary.

sidebar continues on next page

Customer journey maps (or experience maps, as I tend to refer to them—not entirely but mostly a semantic difference) are probably the most useful service design tool I've brought into my user-experience-centric process. I first started using them after initially integrating another service design tool: the service blueprint. When I was working in-house for a company, I found the service blueprint a great way to understand how to *support* the cross-channel experience, especially for an organization with many silos. So it was a great tool for a particular context, but something was missing up front. Service blueprints aren't inherently designed to give insight as to how a journey is *experienced*. I was lacking something earlier in the process that could empathetically illustrate the whole customer experience, which was needed to bring together individual parts of the organization into a singular vision (Figure 5.14). I wasn't deliberately diving into the service design toolkit; I just happened to be looking for a tool, a method, to illustrate the customer journey through a more experiential lens.

There are a few things that I like about customer journey maps. First, it wasn't the map itself, but the *mapping*. When customer journey maps are done right, they involve all the different parts of an organization. The collaborative activity encourages people to get their heads out of the weeds and see the customer experience beyond their silo.

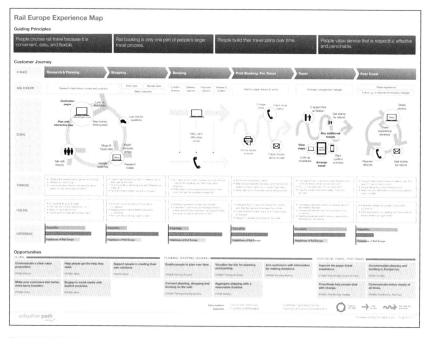

FIGURE 5.14
A customer journey map.

Second, mapping is one of the best ways to identify the changing contexts of a customer's interactions with the company over time. Mapping the journey brings understanding of what customers are *feeling*, *thinking*, and *doing* at any given point in time when they are interacting with a service, and recognition of how that changes.

Third, when done right, maps tell a story with depth and richness around the human experience. I'm a big fan of visualizing stories because visuals are much quicker to comprehend than a few paragraphs. A good model of the journey tells a story through the layering of qualitative and quantitative information. With the element of time, this visual model is the quickest and most effective way to tell a story.

Other traditional user experience tools for connecting different parts of the experience, such as the concept model, lacked the elements of time and context. Scenarios were too focused on a singular part of the experience. User experience methods, at the time, were lacking systems thinking, and customer journey mapping allowed me to take the individual parts and understand how they could be orchestrated together, particularly in this new world that wasn't limited to the digital portion of the experience.

Many instances of past customer journeys I had referenced were in the service of marketing or retail experience. There are examples of customer journey or experience maps out there that are over a decade old. But only in this new age of pervasive connectivity and the convergence of digital and physical experiences are we seeing processes and methods refined, pushed forward, or reinvented altogether.

I apply service design methods in almost every project I do, and I try to explore how to push these methods further—often writing, teaching workshops, and speaking about the practice. But I don't know if I'll ever think of myself as a service designer. Nonetheless, the cross-channel nature of design has meant that I continue to employ a number of service design methods and activities, such as customer journey mapping and service blueprinting, as well as new ways of prototyping, such as acting and business origami, and other tools for understanding the whole system.

I can't say how the vocabulary or semantics will shake out in the end. I think that the best organizations will take user experience—an empathic, outside-in approach to making their customers happy—and not simply think of it as something to apply to their products, but as something that permeates their entire organization. And service design can be an approach, or a set of activities, that we within user experience design can use to bring together a more holistic strategy to defining a great customer experience across channels. What I may call myself in a couple years, or how we'll label our design disciplines, well, we'll leave that to another discussion.

Chris is an experience designer at Adaptive Path. Chris's multidisciplinary approach to design has led to a career spanning information architecture, visual design, and interaction design.

Low Fidelity versus High Fidelity

You now have a completed blueprint that provides an overview of your service in a grid. Our examples above were put together on a computer, but it usually makes sense to create a quick, low-fidelity version first. Sketch out the grid on a big piece of paper or a whiteboard and fill in the touch-points with sticky notes (Figure 5.15), or fill in a simple spreadsheet or table (Figure 5.16). These give you the freedom to move things around, discard things, and generally remain flexible. At some point, you will need a version of the blueprint with more visual polish so that you can incorporate images and sketches. This is likely to take some kind of digital form so that you can easily update and share it (see the sidebar on page 107).

FIGURE 5.15

Using sticky notes on a whiteboard or wall allows you to move things around easily. This method is especially helpful when brainstorming services because sticky notes are impermanent and have limited space to write or sketch the main concept of the touchpoint, which keeps you from getting bogged down with details too early.

FIGURE 5.16

A table or spreadsheet is a fast if visually uninspiring way to get your insights and touchpoint analysis into a digital form.

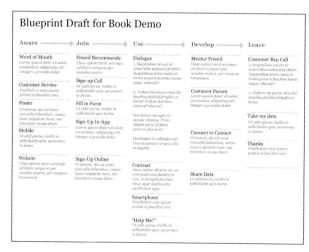

Zooming In and Out

The blueprint is useful for the overarching view, and you need this perspective to make sure you keep all the parts of the service ecology in mind and avoid the silos problem described earlier. During the blueprinting process, however, you will also need to go into more detail than the individual cells allow while still bearing in mind the overall service proposition. This requires mentally zooming in and out from detail to big-picture overview during discussions. For example, what does the print communication look like and how does it fit in with the whole service proposition? How does the desire for a seamless smartphone activity affect the backstage IT requirements? It is exactly these relationships that often get lost in traditional requirements-gathering processes. The blueprint allows you to keep everything connected with a simultaneously user-centered *and* enterprise-centered focus.

As with many design methods, blueprinting is not an exact art. Improvements and tweaks to the process are made from project to project; clients may want specific terminology that matches their internal processes; and agencies develop their own tools and techniques. As we will show in the following chapters, however, the blueprint becomes the backbone of the service design process. It is used for mapping and analyzing the insights research and service ecology as well as designing and developing the service proposition and measuring the results. This makes it an iterative process, of course. The blueprint helps generate ideas but also needs to be changed and updated as new ideas and elements are conceived. Before we go further with the blueprint, however, let us take a look at the service proposition and how to design and develop it.

A Note about Blueprinting Tools

At the time of this writing, no specific tools for creating service blueprints are available. Common design tools range from sticky notes and whiteboards to InDesign and Omnigraffle or Visio. Some service designers use Microsoft Excel due to its ubiquity among clients, especially if they are collaborating on this part of the project. Of course, Excel is far from being a design tool, but it is possible to create clickable links to other spreadsheets or external PDF documents, so the blueprint becomes a kind of map to navigate through the touchpoint details. With some effort, it is also possible to make an Excel blueprint look remarkably well designed. None of these tools is fully satisfactory, because you need the ability to zoom in and out to different levels of detail and to show or hide the different layers. It is important to remember, however, that the tools are not the point of the exercise. Connecting the overview to the details is the aim, so use whatever tools work for you.

Summary

- Services involve many different touchpoint channels and unfold over time. To work through the design of services, you need a way of visually mapping out that complexity.

- You need to be able to mentally "zoom in and out" from the overview of the entire service to the details and back again. A service ecology diagram can help you see the broader context in which a service operates, and a service blueprint helps you structure, design, and align touchpoint interactions as they unfold over time.

- The key activity of service design is aligning what people want to do with the touchpoints they experience frontstage with the backstage business processes that support these activities.

Developing the Service Proposition

If we are looking to improve an existing service, our blueprint has given us a pretty good overview of the component parts of the service and how these are experienced over time. If we are developing something entirely new, we may have less detail but some idea of people's needs and what some of the key touchpoints might be. Before going further into the details and committing significant resources to the project, we need to develop the *service proposition*.

Basing the Service Proposition on Insights

The service proposition is essentially the business proposition, but seen from both the business and the customer/user perspective. It is important that some kind of business model lies behind the service—even if it is a free or public service—otherwise it will not be sustainable or resilient to change. The usual approaches and questions apply: Who is going to fund it? What is the price point and market segment? What do we need to deliver the service, and what will it cost?

The service proposition needs to be based on real insights garnered from the research. For example, is there an unmet need, a gap in the market, an underdeveloped market, a new technology that disrupts existing models, an overly complicated service infrastructure that can be radically simplified, or a changing environment? Any one of these might lead to a business idea and, in turn, a service proposition.

The Zopa Service Proposition

Peer-to-peer lending service Zopa.com (Figure 6.1) is an excellent example of a service proposition based on the insight that companies have a very different relationship to financial services than individual consumers do. One reason for this difference has to do with the way companies are rated by third-party agencies (or the market), which enables companies to present themselves as a viable lending proposition to the financial industry. This system led to the development of the bond market, which allows financial institutions to invest in companies while spreading their risk. This, in turn, allows companies to borrow money in ways not available to consumers, and usually to get a better deal. The Zopa co-founders saw the opportunity to create a similar "bond market" for individuals. A person who may not want to lend £1,000 to one person might be willing to lend £1,000 to be divided among 100 people because the chances of default on the entire amount are very low.

FIGURE 6.1

Peer-to-peer lending service Zopa.com's clear service proposition on their website.

Zopa is also a good example of insight into the power of networks and data as the fuel for disruptive innovation. Behind the scenes, Zopa's proposition is the insight that the data needed to create such a rating system on individuals are out there, but as Zopa co-founder Giles Andrews explained, "Banks have done a fantastic job of telling everyone that they own all this data, which they don't, of course. It's yours, it's mine, it's everybody else's. It certainly doesn't belong to banks, but the industry is structured in such a way that it became very difficult to get that data." [1]

Although individuals can apply to credit rating agencies to get the data held on them, they cannot do much with it. Zopa helps empower individuals by using this data to rate their creditworthiness in a peer-to-peer lending market. Zopa's service proposition is that both lenders and borrowers can

---

1   For more, see Giles Andrews's IPA talk at https://vimeo.com/4843653

get better rates than they would from banks. [2] To do this, Zopa needed to translate their financial thinking into a compelling service and social experience that people could understand and would want to use.

In fact, another opportunity insight for Zopa was the increasing social use of the Internet and the fact that by 2004, when the Zopa founders were starting up, eBay was the biggest online marketplace in the world. Zopa's founders could not explain eBay in any rational economic way. After all, people seemed willing to take the risk of sending money to complete strangers with almost no security, something that a bank would never do. The only way they could explain it was in terms of eBay as a social experience in which people and personal reputations matter.

Zopa is a good example of an organization starting at the people end of the process, asking "What can we do for individuals who do not trust their banks, and how can we build a service business around that?" This is why service design takes a bottom-up, needs-based approach to designing services *with* people.

Returning to the development of the service proposition, it is important when sketching out the ideas at this early stage that the following three questions can be answered:

1. Do people understand what the new service is or does?

2. Do people see the value of it in their life?

3. Do people understand how to use it?

We will revisit these questions in Chapter 7, and add some more as well, but for now let's take a look at these three in turn.

Do People Understand What the New Service Is or Does?

This question may seem obvious, but unlike products, which have physical affordances signaling their potential usage, services can be abstract or even invisible. New services often chart new territory, so explaining what peer-to-peer lending is, to use Zopa as an example, is important. If people are used to borrowing money from banks, they might not understand the point of Zopa. Here is how it is explained on the Zopa website: "At Zopa, people who have spare money lend it directly to people who want to borrow. There are no banks in the middle, no huge overheads and no sneaky fees, meaning everyone gets better rates."

So, now we have a pretty good idea of what the service *does*, but do people want it in their life?

---

2   Zopa stands for "Zone of Possible Agreement"—the overlap between what a person is willing to sell for and another is willing to pay.

Do People See the Value of It in Their Life?

Arguably, the biggest sin designers, engineers, and technologists commit is coming up with stuff they think is cool but nobody actually needs. History is littered with entirely useless products and services. History is also speckled with things people initially thought were useless but that turned out to be things we can hardly live without, such as text messaging, sticky notes, and websites with pictures of cats doing funny stuff.

If you are developing a service proposition, it is essential to think about how it adds value to people's lives. This should, of course, be neatly based on the needs that you uncovered through the insights research, but projects also get steered from above within organizations. Watch out for service propositions that start veering more toward the needs of the business than the customers. The ideal is a proposition that is win-win for both service provider and service user, with each side providing value to the other.

This is how Zopa explained their value: "We hear you ask, 'Why would anyone lend money to a complete stranger?' Because, quite frankly, it gives a better return than saving with a bank. With over £160 [million] lent and a proven track record of managing your money better than banks, we think you should be asking, 'Why not?' "[3]

Many people feel that their bank is a necessary evil that is always trying to rip them off with spurious fees. For this reason, people feel little loyalty toward banks. Zopa confirmed this insight (a pretty obvious one, when you think about it) through their research. People do not trust banks to look after their best interests, but they do trust that their money will be locked up in a big vault somewhere, even if it is just a digital one.

Zopa looked at how they, as a start-up, could compete against this love-hate relationship that customers have with banks. The result was to "go for the soft side of trust," according to Giles.[4] They came up with a tone of voice that is both friendly and straightforward, sometimes funny but not flippant. This guided the design and communication of all their touchpoints: they are as clear and transparent as they can possibly be about how they make money, what the charges are, and what happens if things go wrong. This is the complete opposite of what banks typically do. As Giles explained, "[Banks] have huge amounts of small print. They make their money out of people making small mistakes and they don't make their money out of providing a fair service most of the time." Zopa also emphasized the human side of lending and borrowing money (Figure 6.2), something that many people feel banks have lost sight of.

---

3 As of late 2012, the figure is now more than £230 million lent. Giles Andrews, personal communication, February 13, 2012.

4 The two Giles Andrews quotes in this paragraph are from his IPA talk; see https://vimeo.com/4843653.

FIGURE 6.2

Zopa emphasizes the human stories behind lending and borrowing to differentiate themselves from traditional banks.

So, a combination of the service proposition's underlying principles and how they are communicated across touchpoints helps people understand not only what the proposition is, but the value it has to them. The next thing to tackle is whether they understand how to use it in practice.

Do People Understand How to Use It?

You may have been working on a new service for a while, and the client you are working for should certainly know their business, but do the potential service users understand it? We know how to use a door handle, for example, because we have grown up with them and door handles have physical affordances that encourage us to push, pull, or turn them, but a peer-to-peer thingamabob? Potential users need to have some idea of what "peer-to-peer lending" means, which is why Zopa explain their service as "a marketplace for money." They also explain how their service works, which is more than most traditional banks bother to do (Figure 6.3).

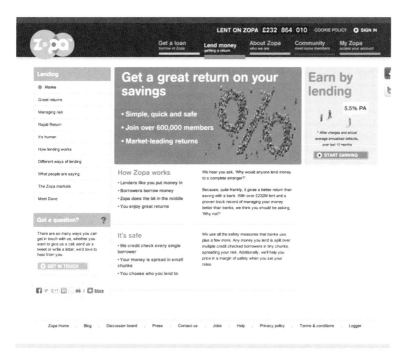

FIGURE 6.3
Zopa clearly explain how their service works in four simple points:
(1) Lenders like you put money in; (2) Borrowers borrow money;
(3) Zopa does the bit in the middle; (4) You enjoy great returns.

So now we know what the service proposition is, understand the value of it
in our lives, and have a rough idea of how it works and how to use it. Zopa is
charting new territory, so they have spent a lot of time and effort detailing
the "how it works" sections of their website to help people understand the
service and build up trust in it, which is central to the business.

Other service propositions can benefit from metaphors and piggybacking
on existing, well-understood products or services. For example, Whipcar is
a peer-to-peer car-sharing service that allows people to rent out their own
cars to strangers when not using them. Because Airbnb, a service that allows
people to rent out a spare room, an apartment, or even a house to strangers
in the same way, was already an established service (Figure 6.4), Whipcar
can describe themselves as "the Airbnb of car sharing" and half the job is
done for them (Figure 6.5). Obviously, people need to know about Airbnb
first, but many of Whipcar's early adopters were also early adopters of other
collaborative consumption sharing services such as Airbnb, so the comparison was well targeted.

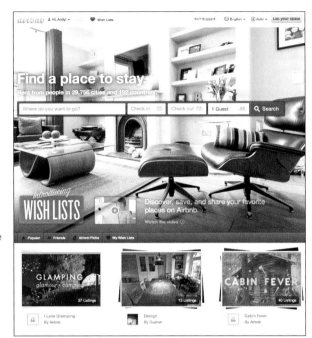

FIGURE 6.4
The "community marketplace for unique spaces," Airbnb makes a clear service proposition on its home page, even through the default text in the form fields.

FIGURE 6.5
Whipcar is a peer-to-peer car-sharing service that is like Airbnb, but for cars. Note the simple three-step "How it works" explanation.

Taking Slices through the Blueprint

You can see in the Zopa example that developing the service proposition requires the constant mental zooming in and out mentioned in Chapter 5. A detail, such as people's trust relationship with conventional banks, leads to the development of a service and business proposition. This proposition has to be communicated back to the users, which means thinking about the detail of the tone of voice across touchpoints.

The service has to make money, so Zopa must take a cut or charge customers in some way. The communication of this element needs to be as clear and transparent as possible because unjust bank fees are part of people's unhappiness with traditional banks. To do this, the Zopa website has a section titled "How we make our money." Every business decision affects the service proposition and the delivery of that proposition. By the same token, details in the touchpoints can affect the entire business. If users do not understand something, such as how and why Zopa take their cut, it will lead to an erosion of trust and Zopa's business will suffer.

The way to manage zooming in and out, from detail to big picture, is to use the service blueprint as a space in which different scenarios can be played out. The blueprint should show the essential parts of the service ecology so that you can track different user journeys through it in a number of "What if?" scenarios. This allows all stakeholders involved in the project—designers, users, staff, and management—to work through all the "If . . . then" decisions that will define the service proposition and experience.

It is at this stage that the real design happens, in the sense of the "coming up with ideas" part of the service design process. Having a blueprint based on solid insights allows the service design team to connect those insights to the business goals and strategy and to design a joined-up experience. The blueprint and other design specification documents ensure that everyone is on the same page.

Choose Where to Focus Resources

Every project has limited resources. Regulatory structures, environmental concerns, and manpower can limit the scope of a project, but most are limited by time and money. Although it would be nice to be able to design every touchpoint perfectly and every conceivable journey through a service, this is usually not possible. You will have to choose which touchpoints to concentrate your efforts on. Choosing a few key touchpoints that express the core of the service is a useful way to get started, whether innovating new services or improving existing ones.

If an existing service is being improved, the obvious touchpoints to work on will arise out of a combination of your insights research (Figure 6.6) and the business strategy. Some will be low-hanging fruit—touchpoints that are currently service fail points, that can easily be redesigned, and that will result in the most significant gains. Some touchpoints, like redesigning a bill, might be an easy graphic design task, but implementing that redesign may be complicated and require all sorts of changes to old and clunky back-end accounting and billing systems. Your low-hanging fruit may not be so easy to pick after all.

If you come from another design discipline, you may be tempted to design the details of touchpoints earlier on in the blueprinting process. Sometimes this can be an entry point into a project. A client may employ you to work on the customer experience of a specific touchpoint, such as a ticket machine interface redesign, but after you have done the insights research you may find that the scope of the service elements that need improvement is much broader. You may find you need to design the entire channel or multiple channels over several phases of the journey.

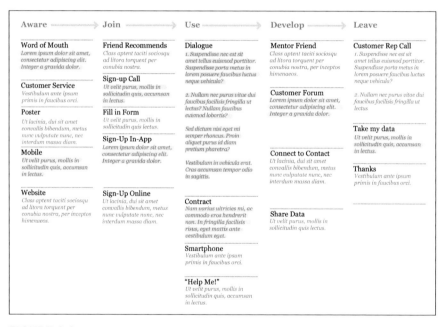

FIGURE 6.6
Insights research may help you decide which touchpoints to focus your resources on. You can highlight or detail these on your blueprint in its early, rough stage.

To avoid ending up with the design process *also* being carried out in silos—with UX or interaction designers working on the screens, product designers working on the products, and so on—you must be clear about where each element fits into the broader context. The way to do this is to zoom out again, look at your blueprint, and design the service proposition, which may mean holding off on the details at first.

The ability to carry both of these levels of detail in your head at once is an essential skill in service design. Although you will mentally zoom in and out, you may find you also need to print out different levels of detail and pin them all up on the wall so that you can discuss them with others working on the project. Here are four useful ways of taking detailed slices through the blueprint.

Journey Summaries

Even for completely new services (and there are very few *really* new services—they are usually modifications, transpositions, or combinations of existing ones), you will need to choose which touchpoints to concentrate the bulk of the effort on. So, how to choose?

Apart from thinking about outcome value versus effort, the easiest way to choose is to track key user journeys through the blueprint. If you have developed personas (real or aggregate ones) from your insights research, you can start imagining how each type of user will move through the service. Mr. Analogue, age 70, might prefer the face-to-face contact channels, whereas Miss Technophile, age 22, might prefer to use online and mobile self-service channels. Typically, most users will experience a mix of channels and may switch between them depending on their context—at work, at home, while traveling, and so on—which is another reason why the coherence *between* the channels is important.

Service designers need to align insights from backstage staff with customer needs. Define where the experience breaks down or great opportunities exist in the customer journey, where channels and technologies play well together to produce value, and when they run counter to each other. Taking journeys through the blueprint is a way to iron out many of these issues (Figure 6.7).

Once you have mapped a particular user's journey across the phases of the service experience and through his or her chosen subset of the touchpoints, you can put together a journey summary. This is essentially a scenario storyboard of each phase of the journey (or steps, if you are looking into finer detail) with a description of what happens and what kind of experience the user should have (Figure 6.8).

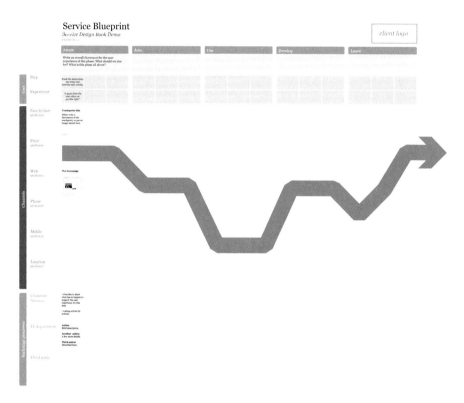

FIGURE 6.7
Tracking a user journey through the blueprint.

FIGURE 6.8
A journey summary describes a particular user's journey through the main service phases, or through a more detailed set of steps. It shows what is going on visually, and the text describes the experiences and interactions with the chosen touchpoints.

Phase and Step Summaries

Apart from allowing you to map journeys across the entire ecosystem of the service, the grid nature of the blueprint allows you to interrogate the rows and columns. Each one of the service phases (Figure 6.9) or steps (Figure 6.10) can be seen as a column that comprises the customer/user experience across all of the touchpoint channels, right through to the backstage stakeholders and activities that are relevant to it.

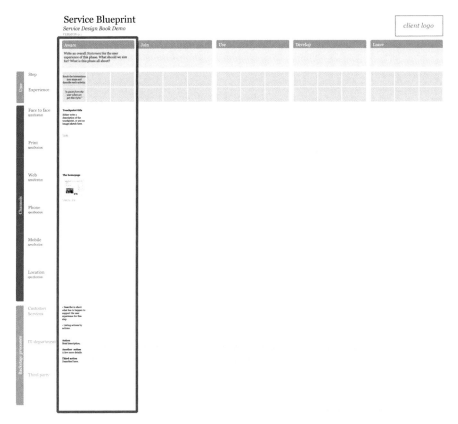

FIGURE 6.9

Each phase is represented by a column that comprises all of the touchpoint channels and the backstage services that support them.

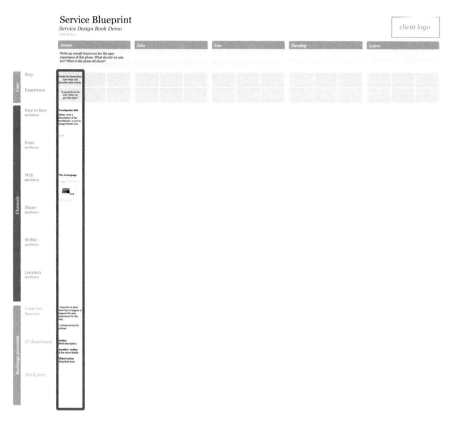

FIGURE 6.10
You can also examine a more detailed step across all the touchpoint channels.

From this you can create a more detailed phase or step summary document that describes what the user experience should be across all the channels at that stage of the journey (Figure 6.11). This summary should also document the connections between different backstage elements of the service and how they need to interact to deliver the required frontstage user experience. It details what kind of experience you want to offer the customer and the implications this has for the technical delivery and business process. You may want to use it to flag certain mission-critical elements or activities.

As with any other interaction or product design, it is important to break down the various interactions into their component elements and map out all of the interactions across all channels. Do third-party services need to be engaged? Do new products or technologies need to be designed and developed? What kind of screen-based interactions are involved? Is the service experience coherent across all these channels? Are parts of the service ecosystem out of your control, and can you mitigate for potential problems here?

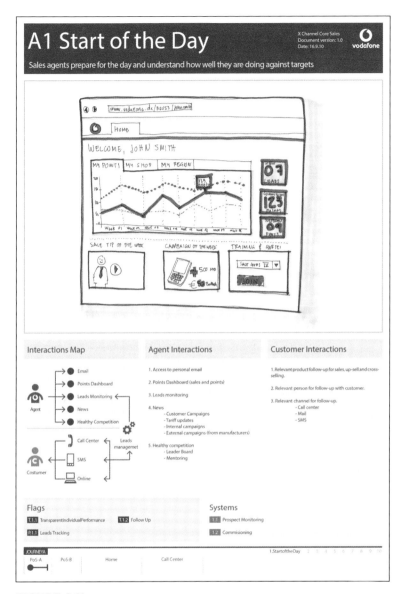

FIGURE 6.11

A phase summary document describes what the user experience should be across channels and what backstage and business elements need to be in place to support it.

For example, joining a service might involve signing up in person, online, or with a mobile phone. This process will probably involve some kind of payment system or registration confirmation response. Other services may include physical elements, such as sending a welcome pack or an access ID card in the mail.

In both the phase and journey summaries, your notes can also include material from your insights research. This may be either what existing users have said about the current service or the needs your insights uncovered that have led to the proposed new service. Moving back and forth between the concept development and the insights research keeps your design process grounded in reality. It is all too easy for ideas to blow out into feature-laden fantasies that people do not actually need, as is often the case with marketing-driven product or service development (we're looking at you, Microsoft Office).

Channel Summaries

If you take a horizontal slice through the service blueprint along the row of a single channel, you can examine how that entire channel works over the life cycle of the service (see Figure 5.12).

This view also allows you to put together a comprehensive specification or briefing document describing the experience of that channel (Figure 6.12). Over several pages, document each moment of interaction with that channel as defined by the phases and steps of the user journey. This specification might be used for a large project, such as the redesign of a service's website, to ensure that the design process does not happen in isolation but, crucially, in the context of the other channel interactions and over time.

Specifying Individual Touchpoints

An individual touchpoint is the intersection of time—the phase or step in the journey—with a channel, such as a customer signing up for a service using a form on a website. In the service blueprint, this is an individual cell (see Figure 5.13), and it describes the what, how, and when of the touchpoint.

 "User registers online" may be a touchpoint, but it is hardly a design brief. You will need to break down each touchpoint into a detailed description so it can be designed or improved (Figure 6.13). This description will form the basis of the briefing and specification document that is passed to other designers and developers to guide their work.

Service Blueprint for trykksaker
Ungdomspakken

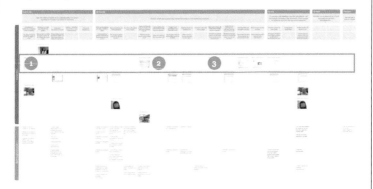

① DM til foreldre som er gjensidigekunder

BESKRIVELSE
Ungdom som fremdeles har folkeregistrert adresse hos sine foreldre er dekket av deres innboforsikring. Derfor kan eksisterende gjensidigekunder kjøpe Alt-i-orden-pakken til barna sine til en lavere pris. Denne DMen skal kommunisere dette som en fordel, slik at pakken oppleves av foreldrene som noe fint man kan gi barna på veien.

FUNKSJONSKRAV
Sendes ut på sensommeren før studiestart.

Evt. legges ved årlig utsendelse av polisedokumenter eller lignende.

Det må klargjøres for mottak av:
- avklippbar svardel med bestilling av pakken
- SMS til 1960 for å bli oppringt av selger

INNHOLD
DMen skal inneholde:
- Et brev med tilbud om Alt-i-orden-pakken og avklippbar svardel
- Ferdigfrankert svarkonvolutt

Brevet skal:
- forklare at Gjensidige har en pakke som inneholder det unge voksne trenger av forsikring- og banktjenester
- forklare at de som gjensidigekunder kan kjøpe denne pakken til lavere pris fordi deres innboforsikring dekker barna, så lenge de ikke melder flytting til folkeregisteret
- kort beskrive fordelene med Gjensidige bank
- kort beskrive forsikringsdekningene som er i pakken
- foreslå at foreldrene kan *gi* denne pakken til sine barn
- gjøre det lett å bestille pakken fra Gjensidige med svardel og ferdig frankert svarkonvolutt
- gjøre det lett å lære med om pakken ved å sende SMS med kodeord ORDEN til 1960

FORM
Bør se ut som vanlig kommunikasjon fra Gjensidige.

FIGURE 6.12

The first page of a channel specification, which describes each phase or step of the user interaction with a specific touchpoint channel. Subsequent pages detail the other touchpoint interactions (2 & 3) highlighted across the channel row.

(se flere skjermbilder: Flash steg 1, Flash steg 2 og hele siden)

BESKRIVELSE
Alt-i-orden er et nytt produkt og trenger en egen side som beskriver pakken og der man kan kjøpe pakken direkte.

FUNKSJONSKRAV
Produktet skal kunne kjøpes på nettet gjennom et skjema på denne siden – ikke gjennom kalkulatorene. Dette skjemaet er en Flash som ligger *på* selve produktsiden.

Skjema i Flash: (Steg 1, Steg 2)
- skal la kunden velge til og fra de dekninger som er valgfrie
- skal kalkulere og vise prisen dynamisk
- bør være i to steg, og be om kontaktinfo i steg 2 for at skjema ikke skal bli avskrekkende langt
- vise priser per år, men oppsummere totalen per måned

Opplysningene fra skjema skal sendes til EDB.

Ved mottatt bestilling skal EDB:
- registrere ny bankkunde
- sende opplysninger direkte inn i S2000 for å registrere ny forsikringskunde
- pakke reisekort og GO3 i pakken og sende den ut i PUM-konvolutt

Bestillingen fra gjensidige.no må merkes slik at
- EDB kan undertrykke ordinær utsendelse av GO3
- Gjensidige forsikring kan undertrykke utsendelse av ordinært reisekort fra S2000
- Kunden får internettrabatt

Side 3 av 7

FIGURE 6.13

A briefing document for an individual Web touchpoint for a youth banking and insurance package launched by Gjensidige.

When you do get to this final level of detail, service design teams are likely to use a range of methods appropriate to the design discipline that the touchpoint involves. Web and mobile interactions require UX wireframes and walkthroughs, products require 3D sketches and renders, connections to IT services require descriptions of database transactions, and print touchpoints may involve everyone from marketing to billing as well as graphic designers and printers. You may also make a storyboard for some kind of time-based communication of the service, such as a video or slideshow with a simple voiceover talking through the service experience over stills or animations that illustrate the stages.

This convergence of skills is probably the most common reason why people from other design and business disciplines perceive service design as the same thing that they already do. At the individual touchpoint level, this is often true. Service design projects draw upon specific expertise where appropriate, and the blueprint and associated material is the design specification for these other capabilities. The difference is that the entire service ecosystem is also designed and connected together. It does not just happen by accident because the various parts are in the same service. The entire purpose of service design blueprinting is to ensure that all the different elements across all touchpoints are not designed in isolation. The blueprint leads to the design specifications for each touchpoint and acts as a way to orchestrate them all. Service design is both broad *and* deep.

Blueprinting is not only an essential service design tool, it is extremely useful when working together with clients as a way to talk about the service concept and how the elements fit together. It breaks down barriers between business units by helping everyone involved in the project understand how his or her part fits into the bigger picture. It also reveals opportunities to join up processes and create more seamless experiences by making sure that there are no gaps in the delivery that everyone thought somebody else was responsible for. Politely ask the client to print out a copy of the blueprint, hang it on the wall, and bring a copy to meetings. [5] It helps.

---

5   Thanks to Anders Kjeseth Valdersnes for this tip.

Summary

Gathering insights to feed into the design of a service is great, but the service also needs to have a business idea behind it—the *service proposition*. Without this, even the best ideas will not be economically viable and sustainable. Key to the service proposition is being able to answer three questions:

- Do people understand what the new service is or does?

- Do people see the value of it in their life?

- Do people understand how to use it?

Taking slices and journeys through the service blueprint allows you to explore whether each touchpoint adequately communicates the answers to these questions from the service user point of view. You can then develop each touchpoint cell in the blueprint into a detailed design specification for the creation of the touchpoint.

CHAPTER 7

Prototyping
Service
Experiences

W hen Ben's six-year-old daughter (Figure 7.1) fell off her bike and bit through half her tongue, he and his wife took her to the local hospital, where the staff did not have the skills to stitch it up, then to the University College London Hospital, where there is a specialist facial injuries team.

FIGURE 7.1
Ben's daughter
experiencing a swing.

At first, the registrar suggested that the operation could be done under local anesthetic, which seemed crazy to Ben, his wife, and the nurse, who clearly had more experience with small children. They then waited for 10 hours while the surgery team worked on a more serious car accident patient before Ben's daughter finally went into the operating room.

It was a short procedure (20 minutes) and the nurse promised to call Ben and his wife when their daughter was out of surgery so they could be there as she came out of the anaesthetic. This did not happen, and they spent an hour or more worrying that something had gone seriously wrong. What had actually happened was that the nurse was on her own and had to stay with Ben's daughter in recovery and was not able to call. Ben's daughter was distraught over the absence of her parents, and all the while they were anxiously pacing nearby. The final happy outcome is that they all went home that night and now there is not even a scar on their daughter's tongue.

Stories like this are common in healthcare, which helps to explain our ambivalence about the word "experience." The experience was terrible but the medical outcome was excellent, and Ben and his wife know which they would prefer. In situations like this, a short-term bad experience is offset by long-term benefit or value. The real problem is in the management of the experience and expectations, and here is where service design can help iron out the kinks.

Defining Experience

The word "experience," and the way it dominates the discussion of service design, feels somewhat unsatisfactory. It may be that the association with such manufactured experiences as a Disney vacation feels like service design is all about entertainment. The idea that we live in an experience economy where we are elevated above the basic needs of food, shelter, and health seems rather too focused on those who are so lucky.

It may also be that "experience" is a somewhat soft term that is difficult to defend against hard factors in services such as economics, operations, or policy. When one thinks about experience as a factor in a hospital, for example, it can be hard to argue for quality of experience when other significant medical matters must take priority.

Working with experiences is to service design what working with communications is to graphic design. The current and future experiences of people—customers, clients, users, patients, consumers—are the context in which service design works. Services can be promoted through positive experiences by ensuring that they meet or exceed users' expectations. The reason experience is important is that, by telling the stories of the people who use or are affected by services, it is possible to either identify opportunities for innovation and improvement or describe future experiences as a way to communicate designs.

Service design is not just about the soft factors, however, such as making people feel good when they enter their hotel room or have a nice chat with someone in a call center. Service design has the ability to contribute to the effectiveness of a service in terms of the hard factors, too—positive economic results, successful operations, or beneficial policy outcomes. Many service design projects have created new revenue streams or boosted existing businesses.

Getting the experience right means gaining customer loyalty so that people are less likely to switch to another company. They are also more likely to recommend your service to someone else, doing your promotion work for you. In noncommercial contexts, people often have no option but to use a particular service, such as the tax office or unemployment services. The fact that users are locked in to using a service is not a reason to neglect their experiences, but all the more reason to make sure they experience something positive and engaging because they cannot escape it. This can make all the difference in a patient's recovery of health or the uptake of a public policy.

There is some contention about whether one can even design an experience because it is obviously something that happens inside someone else's mind and body. Of course, designers cannot really dictate people's exact experiences, but anyone who has been absorbed in a film, novel, or amusement park experience, or who has been bullied or tried to make someone laugh, knows that experiences can be created in people by other people.

Designers can design the *conditions* for an experience, and one can see the importance of experience in many aspects of design, ranging from the UX design of digital interfaces to the broader context of design employed by the National Health Service in their experience-based design toolkit. [1]

Although experiences are a crucial element to understand and consider in service design, they are one of a number of factors alongside economics, operations, and domain expertise. It is the combination of all of these that comprise the entire service proposition, with the service user as an organizing "common ground" around whom all aspects of the service can focus.

Types of Experience

In a service design context, it helps to ask questions about what kinds of experiences we are talking about. Are we talking about *task* experiences—the experience of trying to get something done? Are we talking about *commercial* experiences—the experience and how it reflects our perception of value? Or are we talking about *life* experiences—the experience that shapes our wider quality of life?

We can break these down into the following four categories:

- User experience: interactions with technologies

- Customer experience: experiences with retail brands

- Service provider experience: what it is like on the other side

- Human experience: the emotional effect of services (e.g., healthcare) that impact quality of life and well-being

This is not an exhaustive list, but these are the main ones we want to take into account when designing services. Together they cover almost all of the aspects and interactions in services that are important to be aware of and consider in design. We have made a distinction between "user" and "customer"

---

1   NHS Institute for Innovation and Improvement, "The EBD Approach," www.institute.nhs.uk/quality_and_value/introduction/experience_based_design.html.

experiences because there are many situations in which users are not customers. Nurses are an obvious example because they are using services but are not paying customers. Nurses are also service providers, so roles frequently overlap, which is why the frontstage/backstage metaphor does not always work well. In many situations, such as someone browsing a website for research, people are users but not customers. In self-service scenarios, users and customers are the same thing, as we will describe below.

User Experience

UX design is a subject we expect many readers to be familiar with, so we do not try to redefine it here. We relate it mainly to task-based experiences, although in many situations these affect the commercial and life quality experiences, too.

An individual's ability to complete tasks within a service can be crucial to the success of a service. The way that tasks are designed can have a significant impact on the effectiveness of the service as a whole, and tasks within a service are commonly redesigned in ways that increase service performance or revenue. In many situations, confusing wording, layout, or basic user interface design causes users to give up and try a different touchpoint channel or even a different service all together.[2]

Web-based services have pioneered a focus on user experience as an essential component of the way they operate. Google are able to evaluate how different shades of blue in links influence click-through rates on search results. This usability approach, based on understanding how well people can achieve their goals, is valuable and is applied by designers to a range of contexts, from shopping to city navigation.

In the context of a task-based activity, the experience of using a service is manifested in the sense of using a tool. Individuals are generally trying to use the tangible elements of a service, such as signage, interfaces, and communications, as they attempt to complete everyday tasks such as finding a train platform, buying tickets, or understanding the fare choices.

We suggest that user experience in this context is primarily concerned with tasks, short time frames, and interactions with nonhuman touchpoints.

Customer Experience

You may have clients whose main goal is to improve the experience their customers have when using services. This goal would seem to be an obvious thing for companies to want to achieve, but they are often more engaged in

---

2   In Luke Wroblewski's *Web Form Design* (www.rosenfeldmedia.com/books/webforms/), Jared Spool gives an astounding account of a single button on a website that made a $300 million difference to one online retailer's sales.

trying to make internal efficiencies and savings. To many companies, customers are just like any other part of the business, a resource to be managed.

Companies that do want to improve customer experience are not just dealing with soft factors. They calculate that such changes will increase the amount customers use and pay for their services in the first place, as well as reduce the number of customers who choose to take their custom elsewhere. Churn, as the turnover of customers between competing service providers is called, is a costly business. New customers must be persuaded to replace those who leave, which is generally more expensive than retaining existing ones.

Customer experience is in some senses the sum of the task experiences involved in using a service. If users are constantly frustrated when trying to complete goals and tasks, then they may leave and go elsewhere, and it only takes one or two poorly considered touchpoints for this to happen. This much is obvious, but customer experience is something more than a happy/unhappy binary dynamic.

As customers, we have expectations of a service in terms of quality and value that overarch the day-to-day tasks we undertake. These expectations are set by the brand and our experience of other services, and are closely tied to the amount we are paying. Consider budget airlines compared to premium air travel—the brand promise of each sets our service expectations. If our experience does not match our expectations, we are disappointed and become more likely to switch next time. In this case, the emotion of bad service is not just frustration but also a reflection on the quality we are getting for our money. We might hate the service on a budget flight (most people do), but it is exactly what we were promised when we booked the cheap ticket. Obviously, the ideal situation is for even cheap services, such as a budget airline, to have good service. The danger in cutting service quality as a cost-saving measure is that the race to the bottom is very quick indeed. Many other businesses can structure themselves to compete on price, in which case quality of service becomes the point of difference. Quality of service tends to be part of a company's culture, and culture is much harder to restructure once it has been set.

In many respects, the management of customer experience is about managing the delivery of the service and customer expectations against what is actually delivered. "Customer experience" feels like an odd term to apply to public sector services such as education or healthcare, however. Nevertheless, it is a term more and more in use in public organizations as they find that they are compared to their commercial counterparts and that expectations have been set by politicians or others not directly engaged in having to provide the service.

Customer experiences are longer term than user experiences but generally have some limits to them, such as contractual limits on car rentals, phone plans, and insurance. You might have a positive or negative user experience when trying to enter credit card details for payment on Amazon, for example, but your customer experience encompasses a range of such smaller, task-based interactions. The customer experience is the total sum of a customer's interactions with a service.

Service Provider Experience

Although they have shorter time spans, user experience and customer experience are still important aspects of any service design. In many cases, service experiences are co-produced by the customer and their interactions with a touchpoint, such as using a ticketing machine or speaking to a staff member. In these scenarios, the *user* experience and *customer* experience may be the same thing. If someone cannot operate a self-service check-in machine in an airport but no staff are available at the check-in counters, then the poor kiosk touchpoint user experience is also a poor customer and service experience.

One of the ways in which service design differs from UX design or customer experience design is that it is not just focused in one direction. Although the backstage/frontstage metaphor is often used in service design projects and blueprints, this metaphor can fall apart in many situations because it focuses on front-end, customer-facing experiences only.

A useful way of thinking about people's roles in services is to think of every exit "off stage" as an entrance somewhere else. This is particularly true in situations in which the staff involved in delivering the service are service users and service providers at the same time.

To expand on our previous example, a nurse provides a service in at least two directions—to the patient and to the doctors. She may also provide services to the hospital administration and health insurance companies. At the same time, she is using internal hospital services (e.g., IT systems, catering, and security services), commercial laboratory services, and other sources of information (e.g., ambulance drivers, other nurses, literature, flyers, and databases).

In addition, the patient and the relatives or carers of the patient also provide information and, in some cases, services for nurses. When Andy's two-year-old daughter broke her arm during a family vacation in Italy (our daughters do seem rather accident prone), the nurses made ample use of Andy's friend who could speak Italian instead of calling on the services of an interpreter.

Here is where the customer/user nomenclature starts to fall apart. What do we call a nurse? She is not a customer, nor is she a user—these words and ways of thinking about how to design for her needs do not go far enough. Actor-network theory would have us call her an actor, or we could refer to her as an agent, but perhaps to think of her simply as a person in a *role* who has interactions in both directions is the easiest way to design for her.

Human Experience

Our experience with examining and designing service interactions between staff and customers has shown us that people see straight through things that are meant to be personal in a customer service contact if they are not really personal. A personalized mailing that is clearly a form letter is one obvious example that we mentioned in Chapter 1. Less obvious is someone reading through a script while pretending to be interested in and engaged with the customer, but without any emotional investment in the exchange. If staff do not really care, but just go through the motions of doing so, we feel a disconnect on a human level.

As Ben and Andy's hospital stories illustrate, some service experiences are not primarily about tasks or customers but go much deeper and touch our emotions much more significantly. Most people experience this in long-term public services such as education or healthcare. When we interact with them, we feel there are tasks to be completed successfully, of course, but we also have a sense of the right to feel that there should be value in the delivery of these services because they impact who we are and our sense of ourselves. When teaching is reduced to cost savings on a per pupil basis, it misses the point of education. Human experience contains a huge range of emotions—pride, embarrassment, shame, euphoria, despair, joy, depression, love, hate—as well as the feelings elicted by smaller, everyday experiences, such as a child's first word, a promotion at work, or even just a friendly inter-action with a stranger.

As service designers start to apply their skills in personal, public, and social projects, it is essential that they consider the impact the service has on people and their sense of who they are. If things go wrong at the level of the human experience, the result is not just frustration or a simple economic equation—damage to a brand image or a missed sale—but something that affects the development of people's lives.

These kinds of human experiences are often longer term, but they may comprise short experiences that stay with people for a lifetime. Education is again a good example. Most people have some memory of being either finally understood or unfairly misunderstood by a particular teacher. These are experiences that continue to affect people positively or negatively into their adult lives.

The human impact of services is also important to the brand experience and the bottom line in commercial services. A bad experience during a hotel stay or a conversation with a phone company's call center is irritating and likely to lead to customers shopping elsewhere in future. In public services, such as healthcare, transportation, welfare, or energy, the human experi-ence is essential because often no alternatives are available to the users of that service. Sadly, many of those services operate as a government-run monopoly in which there is little incentive to improve service and great pressure to cut costs. Service designers cannot single-handedly change the world, but they can offer a set of methods and approaches to help bridge the gap between service systems and human value.

Though the task of stitching up Ben's daughter's tongue was completed successfully and Andy's daughter leaving the hospital in Genoa with her arm in plaster meant her stay there was over, clearly the impact on both families was long lasting. Going home with patched-up daughters helped us put the trauma behind us, but it showed us how, in other cases, a lack of attention to the human experience could be much more damaging and permanent.

The roles in these service scenarios are also much less clear cut because the service participant is much more involved in the service, unlike the clarity of being a customer. This is why thinking in terms of time spans—short term and long term—as well as the personal and global context of a service are critical to the service designer's mindset when designing service experiences.

Expectations versus Experiences

Product experience is about the quality of tangibility. The fundamental concept to embrace when you design a service is that *perceived quality* is defined by the gap between what people expect and what they actually experience. [3] Therefore, the primary focus for a service designer is to make sure that every interaction with the service sets the right level of expectation for the next interaction. It means that the level of quality and the nature of the experience need to be the same over time and across touchpoints.

This idea that the curve of the experience should be flat often runs contrary to conventional marketing wisdom that tends to look for "moments of truth," and to the ideals of designers who constantly strive to create the ultimate experience. In fact, when you exceed expectations at a certain point, you have already set yourself up to disappoint at the next interaction if you cannot deliver at the same level. Sometimes, you may need to consider reducing the quality of a certain touchpoint to enhance the overall experience of quality in the service. When you set consistent expectations in each interaction and fulfill them in the next, people will feel quality.

If the way people accessed services was completely linear and predictable, the ups and downs could be managed like in a movie or a theme park ride, but this is tricky to achieve in a service. Customers choose their own speed and path through a service, so you can only minimize the gap between expectation and experience by securing consistency. This goes for language, visual design, interaction design, and product design.

---

3   The theory behind the gap between expectation and experience is outlined in more detail in Valarie Zeithaml, A. Parasuraman, and Leonard L. Berry, *Delivering Quality Service: Balancing Customer Perceptions and Expectations* (New York: Free Press, 1990).

Even more important, backstage consistency is crucial to success. CRM systems must be designed so call center staff can feel reassured that they are using the same language that website customers have in front of them. The mobile plan must look the same when customers buy it online and when they receive the first bill. Billboard ads for a bank must tell the same story that people experience when they use the bank's mobile app.

Great service experiences happen when all touchpoints play in harmony, and when people get what they expect day after day. This is the baseline and it may sound a bit boring and joyless when described this way. What we are arguing, though, is that even this baseline level of designing and delivering services that "just work" is challenging, which is why so many services are awful experiences. Almost no company or organization achieves this level, which is why it needs to be measured and modified over time (see Chapter 8).

Keeping a minimal gap between expectations and experiences, rather like tram lines tracking closely next to each other, does not mean that there is no scope for surprise and delight. But things surprise and delight us because they are *unexpected*.

The smallest expectation-experience mismatch with a touchpoint can ruin any overblown efforts to pump up the experience artificially. Imagine a luxurious hotel stay with a big basket of fruit in your room and friendly and efficient staff. Now imagine you see a lipstick mark on the glass in the bathroom or dust on the bedside table. You immediately assume all the other "luxury" elements are just window dressing for a flawed backstage process, and that corners are being cut on these services. The magic spell is broken and everything else comes across as a cynical attempt to get you to pay more than you should, like the $10 bottle of water on the sideboard. It no longer feels personal, and it would have been better for the hotel to offer a low-key but clean and honest experience. Yet, something simple, such as a handwritten welcome note or a genuine communication, can provide unexpected delight because it not only feels, but *is*, personal.

Considering Time as an Object of Design

For service designers, the objects of design are experiences over time, although describing it this way may seem rather disingenuous because service design is not an abstract activity. It is very grounded in the materials that make up a service, including chairs, posters, buildings, machines, and interfaces. There is a serious, if subtle, point of difference to take account of, though. The shift in mindset is that these objects are no longer the subject of design, they are the features. They may or may not be used by the customer, and they will change in independent and interdependent ways as the service evolves. The service designer needs to focus on how these elements come together over short or long periods of time, and the designer needs to help orchestrate or direct their assembly.

There are two different ways to look at time when you want to design a better experience: relationship time and frequency.

Relationship time is what is represented in the customer journey. It means that you want to design the experience to be relevant to people who are at different stages in their relationship with the service. Although this is an obvious point, in many services people's expectations are mismanaged because the provider does not consider the fact that some people have had more time to become familiar with the service than others.

For instance, when Oslo University Hospital wanted to develop better patient information, they initially completely underestimated what a challenge it was for patients to figure out where to park the first time they came to the hospital. Finding parking created more uncertainty and irritation for people than not understanding exactly what was in a drug they were prescribed. Long-term patients had exactly the opposite concern. This is why the customer journey and service blueprint are such important tools for integrating the experience over time in a service.

Frequency of interaction is a different consideration when you design services. Some service experiences, such as news services or train schedules, work well with a high frequency of interactions. Other services, such as paying tax, are best when they interact with people with low frequency and visibility. The frequency of communication with a service is something that needs to be described in detailed design specifications and will vary from service to service and touchpoint to touchpoint. We have all experienced services that steal our time by getting in touch with us when we least need them, as well as services that we wish responded faster and when it was most relevant. Designing the appropriate frequency is a task that requires subtlety, testing, and monitoring over time.

Service Experience Prototyping

Why Prototype?

When developing a service, you can save the organization large amounts of time and money if you design and test the experience before resources are spent on designing the processes and technology needed to eventually run the service. Therefore, it is important to create an environment in which you can involve real people with trying the service as early as possible in the development process.

Service providers will tell you that the devil is in the details when it comes to delivering successful services in an efficient way. Sometimes, seemingly small problems can have a huge effect on the customer experience. Unclear instructions or inconsistent language on interfaces can cause unintended problems or complete failure to use the service, for example, but even small irritations can be enough of a barrier to prevent people from bothering to switch from their old way of doing things to using a new service. The challenge is that experiences are often hard to rationalize and explain in the abstract. People need to experience a service or touchpoint before they can tell you what does not work and what really makes a difference.

Because a new service can provide people with an experience they have never had before, it is important to make it real and tangible. If you ask people to imagine a new service, they tend to become analytical and problem-oriented. On the other hand, when people are allowed to experience a working prototype—something tangible that contains the key elements of the touchpoints and flow of the service interactions—they may react to the performance rather than the abstract concept.

Prototyping Is the Willing Suspension of Disbelief

Unlike a product prototype, which is an object people can hold in their hands to get a sense of how it feels, service prototypes need to be experiences of interacting with multiple touchpoints as well as taking into account how those experiences unfold over time and in context.

Because service designing uses theatrical metaphors for blueprinting, it makes sense to think of experience prototyping as theater. In a theater, one typically finds a stage, some actors with different roles and goals, some props, and a script. The combination of these allows people to act out situations that are not necessarily real, but the result is a believable (and often, enjoyable) experience.

You can use experience prototyping to co-design a new service. This means the prototype exists both as a "live sketching tool" used to conceive concepts, details, and ideas, but also as a way to verify or disprove any theories you have while creating the service.

Here are some questions to consider while experience prototyping, which expand on the three questions asked in Chapter 6. You should always look for ways to improve each of these during the prototyping phase.

1. Do people understand the service—what the new service is or does?

2. Do people see the value of the service in their life?

3. Do people understand how to use it?

4. Which touchpoints are central to providing the service?

5. Are the visual elements of the service working?

6. Does the language and terminology work?

7. Which ideas do the experience prototype testers have for improvement?

Experience prototypes enable you to gain a level of insight that is deeper than you could possibly achieve by observing and interviewing people alone. It gives you feedback on the details of the proposition and touchpoints that sometimes lead directly into the final detailing and build of the design.

Four Levels of Experience Prototyping

Experience prototypes can range from quick and dirty to elaborate stagings over longer periods of time. We generally divide these levels into four types of prototyping: an inexpensive, semistructured discussion; a walkthrough participation; a more elaborate simulation; and a full-scale pilot (Figure 7.2). Usually, a mix of elements from the four types creates an effective level of prototype testing. Of course, the budget increases with the increasing detail of each level, so you may find each stage of prototyping allows the client to sign off on the next step.

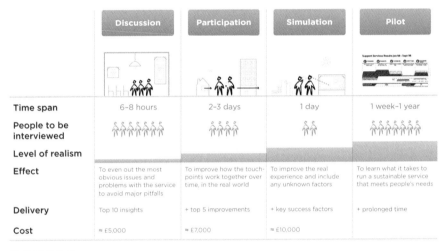

	Discussion	Participation	Simulation	Pilot
Time span	6–8 hours	2–3 days	1 day	1 week–1 year
People to be interviewed				
Level of realism				
Effect	To even out the most obvious issues and problems with the service to avoid major pitfalls	To improve how the touchpoints work together over time, in the real world	To improve the real experience and include any unknown factors	To learn what it takes to run a sustainable service that meets people's needs
Delivery	Top 10 insights	+ top 5 improvements	+ key success factors	+ prolonged time
Cost	≈ £5,000	≈ £7,000	≈ £10,000	

FIGURE 7.2
The four levels of experience prototyping.

Discussion

A discussion prototype is very similar to a user insight interview, and is usually the most affordable option. You can bring a series of touchpoint mock-ups to a one-hour interview and discuss them according to your planned user journey. The role of the people you are interviewing is to be themselves, react to the touchpoints, and offer feedback as if the interactions were real.

The effect of discussion is to iron out the most obvious issues or problems with the service proposition and to avoid major pitfalls. A typical discussion prototype involves between 5 and 10 customers and delivers insights that will help you refine the design. This can be extremely useful when trying to work out what the service proposition should be. You can mock up different website pages or marketing materials, for example, to see how people react to the different propositions. They may react to pricing, particular service elements, or not understand what you are trying to pitch at all. All of this input is useful during the concept development.

Participation

For participation prototypes, an interview similar to the discussion proto-type is carried out, but it is done in the environment where the service is expected to take place. You provide the customer with tangibles at physical locations, and involve staff from the service provider to deliver service. For instance, you could involve a call center, sales division, help desk, or office and shop staff using mock-up print materials or screens to see how they react to them.

The aim of participation prototypes is to improve how the touchpoints work together when you add to the equation the elements of the service unfolding over time and in a real location. You can learn more about which interactions are critical for the service and also understand what people actually do, rather than what they say they do. A typical participation prototype involves between two and six customers and enables you to define detailed insights and improvements to the design.

Simulation

A simulation prototype is a combination of the first two types of proto-typing above, but in more detail. For a simulation, you might recruit fewer customers but provide them with a full-scale prototype of the service with more finished-looking touchpoints than the mock-ups used in a partici-pation prototype. This requires more preparation, and depending on the service, you might need some sort of controlled environment for running the prototype. This means you can prepare touchpoints for the real locations in which they will be used, such as a department store, a customer information center, or inside a bus or a train, for example.

In a simulation, you add a longer period of time to the mix. You may work with customers over a period of days or weeks to see how people's experi-ence develops as they go through a series of interactions. You can test how the experience builds when people move between touchpoints and develop familiarity with the service offering.

The effect of a simulation prototype is to understand how to improve touch-points, and the way they work over time. Instructional elements might be useful at first, for example, but then soon become annoying if users cannot bypass them easily once they are familiar with the service. In addition, you are likely to discover one or more "X factors" that were impossible to know about before the design got to this level of detail. Sometimes these can be critical to the success of the service, such as the wording of a button or an awkward physical placement of a touchpoint.

A typical simulation prototype involves between two and six customers. Two or three is more common because of the budget involved, but if you can afford it, go for more. The simulation prototype enables you to share detailed insights with the development team and define improvements and key success factors for the service experience.

Pilot

If the service you are working with is at a level where infrastructure and manpower is available, you can launch a pilot. This level of prototyping is not simulating the experience but actually delivering it to the end users. Through sustained delivery of a near-finished service, you can learn what works and what does not when trying to meet the needs of real customers. A pilot prototype is a beta service and needs to support iterative improve-ments throughout its life span so that you are able to try new approaches to problem solving.

The aim of a pilot is to learn what works for a larger group of customers, over a longer period of time, and what sort of resources need to be allocated for the service. Public services, such as employment schemes, often affect end users over months and years (see the Make It Work case study in Chapter 9, for example). A pilot can generate systematic evidence for a new service design and can gather proof that a good business case exists for the solution and that customers or users gain sustained and improved value from the service.

Preparing for Experience Prototyping

Obviously, the exact level of detail you will require in terms of mock-ups, props, locations, and people will vary from project to project due to time and budget considerations, but three key steps are necessary at every level.

Step 1—The Customer Journey

Develop one or more customer journeys that describe the situations you would like to act out with customers. It can be valuable to consider every step from "Aware" to "Leave" (Figure 7.3). This provides you with feedback on parts of the whole life cycle of the new service. Is it easy to understand the new service and how people buy into it? If they need to change something or stop using the service, how does that work?

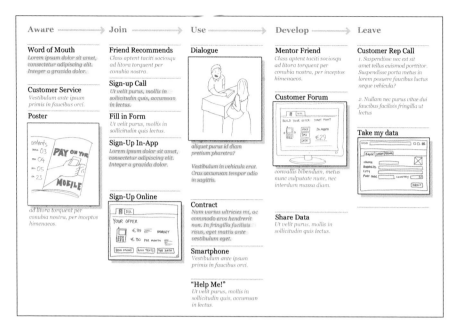

FIGURE 7.3
A basic text blueprint with key touchpoints highlighted, ready to be mocked up for prototyping.

The user journey acts as the manuscript for the prototype and should describe the different actors and which tangibles are needed. Here you can return to your blueprint of the entire service and combine it with the insights into the users that you gained in the research phase. You can then decide to take a particular kind of user through a journey using specific touchpoints you have created for the experience prototype.

Step 2—People

Participants

When recruiting people to participate in a prototype, first consider whether you need any help from the service provider, your client. Do you need staff with specific skills or knowledge about the company, product, or service?

Next, you need to recruit potential customers. Do this the same way you would recruit for a user insight interview. Recruit people with relevant demographics or people at different stages in the service journey so that they can play roles in the different phases of the customer journey (Figure 7.4).

FIGURE 7.4
Prototyping for a Transport for Oslo project: hand sketches on an iPad for a new ticket machine (left) and signage posters (right).

Roles

To enable participants to act out the prototype, you need to define their roles clearly. You should ask them to play themselves, but it helps to give them some detail on their role in terms of context. For example, ask a hospital patient to play herself before she fell ill, or ask a customer of a bank to imagine he has used the service for years.

Goals

The other thing to remember when briefing participants is to give them a goal or an outcome for their interactions with the service. For example, ask them to get through town using the bus and a new map, or get a doctor to prescribe a new medicine. As in theater, the character's goals are essential to creating an interesting drama. As such, you should ensure that the goals you set participants will show up potential problems with the service.

Step 3—Tangibles

Create tangible artifacts for the central interactions you want to stage, and decide on the level of quality and realism you need them to have. For some prototypes, it is sufficient to have hand-drawn sketches or computer print-outs; for others you might need click-throughs or live mock-ups running on a computer. Design the tangibles and test them as part of a journey internally among the project team before you prototype in a live context. The participants are spending their time testing your work, and even if they are being paid, it is tedious if your prototypes are too unreliable.

It is important to remember the purpose of the prototypes. There is little point in prototyping something that you know will work. A Web service registration that uses a standard sign-up form and confirmation e-mail format probably does not warrant prototyping, unless some aspect of it has come up in the insights research that suggests it is a service-critical problem.

You should aim to prototype elements that are critical to the service experience or are unknowns and hard to gauge as experiences until you try them out. These elements warrant being prototyped in higher fidelity than other parts of the service (Figure 7.5). For example, if you are prototyping a ticket machine and the on-screen flow is the most important thing, then mocking this up on an iPad and holding it in front of someone will give you a good idea of how well it works in context. On the other hand, perhaps the physical redesign of the ticket machine is more important to increase accessibility, in which case you may want to spend more time on a foam-core mock-up of the kiosk itself and try it out on location with a participant in a wheelchair.

FIGURE 7.5
High-fidelity mock-ups of forms, letters, and brochures that customers engaged with over a week to simulate the process of buying a new insurance policy.

Experience Prototyping Practicalities

Consider the tools you will need to document and run the prototype. You will typically want to take pictures, or use mobile phones to send messages or set up phone conversations. Here are some useful tricks for designing quick and effective prototypes.

Listening In on Call Center Prototyping

Design a script and materials for the customer. Place one researcher with the customer and one with the call center staff member (Figure 7.6). Observing how the conversation develops from both sides will help you understand what the customer needs as well as what staff need to deliver good service. Make sure you give the customer the direct number of the call center staff member your researcher is sitting with.

FIGURE 7.6
A researcher with a customer and another with a call center staff member listen in and observe both sides of a sales call to see how users respond to the prototyped tools and materials.

Make Websites in Microsoft Excel

If you need to test website forms, you can easily build formulas and visualize data in Excel. Dress it up as a website and paste a browser frame around it, and you have an advanced Web prototype built in a few hours.

Cheap Modular Furniture

If you need to test the dynamics of a physical environment, stores like IKEA can provide most of the components you would need to try out different layouts of physical environments with a realistic level of detail. If you build up a collection of props and reuse them, it can be cheaper than building mock-up elements from foam core each time. For very rough mock-ups acted out within the project team, you can use cardboard boxes rescued from local stores.

Online Prototyping Blogs

Blogging platforms such as Wordpress, Textpattern, and MovableType are a quick and easy way to put together insights material for everyone to access and comment upon (see "Insights Blogs" in Chapter 4), but they are also useful for setting up quick Web prototypes and/or capturing feedback on a service. If you have good in-house Web talent, you might want to put something together quickly from scratch, but it is often easier to modify a basic blog template if you just want to get across the overall service proposition rather than the specific user interface or usability (Figure 7.7). Of course, a prototype might become as refined as a nearly finished beta website, which would be a properly crafted affair.

FIGURE 7.7
A website for Surebox using a blogging platform to run the prototype.

For beta phases, users are recruited and given access to a service at an early stage of its final development for a specified period of time, say six weeks. They are asked to use the service and provide feedback through a blog on how it performs.

Online prototyping provides fresh input beyond the original insights research from users, which helps inform designers about usability, clarity, and desirability. Once the improvements are carried out, users are again asked to provide feedback in an iterative process.

Keep in touch with users at regular intervals throughout the process to encourage them to participate and provide support if required. An incentive such as cash or a voucher can be offered for each piece of feedback recorded.

This technique is useful for uncovering usability problems, and a heavily Web-based service would need proper usability testing and expertise on board, but in the early stages a quick prototype can clarify what the service is and what additional uses it may have other than those anticipated.

Summary

When services are consistent across touchpoints and time, they deliver great experiences. When designing service experiences, keep the following in mind:

- Design for time and context.

- Design the links between touchpoints with the same care as the touchpoint itself.

- Set consistent expectations in each interaction, and fulfil them.

- Design for the experience of both users and staff.

To find out whether your service design hangs together as a coherent experience, create some prototypes. Often the "feel" of the service touchpoints does not become apparent until somebody tries to use them. When prototyping services, be sure to include the following steps:

- Define customer journeys to act out.

- Define participants' roles and goals.

- Design tangibles/touchpoints.

- Set up additional tools and infrastructure.

- Role-play the service experience in a real context.

CHAPTER 8

Measuring Services

S ervice designers and service providers both have a need to prove that design provides a return on investment. Results can be measured in terms of money made or saved, in an improved customer or user experience, value created to society, or reduced drain on the environment.

We have not found a single, perfect method of measurement that provides robust evidence for the value of service design. However, it is important to define *some* measurement criteria before a new design is launched and to track these parameters to prove value and improve the service. You will do yourself and the field of service design a great favor if you always include the definition of performance indicators in your proposals. Exactly what to measure is likely to vary with each new service design.

In the industrial age, leaders like Henry Ford and General Motors' Alfred Sloan developed science-based corporate measurement systems to enable them to "manage by the numbers." It soon became apparent, however, that this approach lacked the systems approach needed to ensure quality and improve performance on a continual basis. [1]

After World War II, W. Edwards Deming, an American statistician and management guru, pioneered a more systems-based approach that first proved its effectiveness in the Japanese automotive industry. In the 1990s this came to be known as "lean" enterprise or production—a focus on removing every tiny inefficiency from manufacturing processes. Many enterprises in the service sector use "lean" as an approach to improve their services, but this method flourished in the industrial tradition, and although it may make service delivery more efficient, it rarely improves the customer experience. Ironically, Deming himself argued that a myopic focus on efficiency and the elimination of product defects was not enough. Instead, companies should try to predict the underlying customer *needs* and think about what products or services will be required 5 to 10 years from the present and innovate for that future. [2] Measuring efficiencies in production makes sense from an industrial point of view, although the sustainability agenda requires companies to consider the full life cycle of products. But for services, what must be measured is *consumption*—the experiences of the service provider's agents and users. [3]

When you base measurement on the problems and successes people have when they *use* a service, you are better positioned to streamline delivery while improving the customer experience. Efficiency and experience are rarely contradictory forces, as long as you use the customer experience as

---

1 John Seddon, *Freedom from Command and Control: A Better Way to Make the Work Work* (Buckingham, UK: Vanguard Consulting Ltd, 2003).

2 W. Edwards Deming, *The New Economics for Industry, Government, Education*, 2nd ed. (Cambridge, MA: MIT Press, 2000).

3 James P. Womack and Daniel T. Jones, "Lean Consumption," *Harvard Business Review*, March 2005, http://hbr.org/2005/03/lean-consumption/ar/1.

a baseline for measurement, because improved efficiency usually goes hand in hand with happier customers.

As an example, insurance customers will tell you that they highly value quick payment when they make a claim. When insurers meet this customer need, they find that they save processing time because customers do not require as many interactions. They also find that people are likely to submit lower claims. The quicker an insurance company settles a claim after a burglary, the fewer CDs people seem to find missing. Happy corporation, happy customers.

Another advantage of measuring from the outside in is that it enables companies to compare themselves to the competition in a more accurate way. They will not be able to get call center response time numbers from their competition, but it is as easy to speak with a competitor's customers as with their own. Do their competitor's customers get through on the phone more quickly than their own customers?

Starting with the customer makes as much sense for measurement as it does for design.

Measurement for the Common Good

Measurement is traditionally seen as a way for managers to control and plan their businesses better. Over the last decade, however, digital systems have made data radically cheaper to harvest and more accessible to managers, frontline staff, and customers. This democratization of data means that the purpose of measurement is shifting away from simply providing management tools. Measurement becomes a way to engage managers, frontline staff, and customers in collaborative service improvement. When measurement becomes transparent, there is an opportunity to make improvement a common cause, not a driver of adversity.

Good feedback channels for customers enable them to tell service providers about problems and opportunities. Customer ratings and purchasing patterns enable customers to make better choices based on other people's experiences. The same measures set a standard for both managers and staff to live up to. When this is bolstered with internal business data, managers and staff can work better together to meet customer needs and drive efficiency.

Before we get into which data are useful to measure, it is worth emphasizing that the act of measuring in itself is as important as what you measure. Most managers will say that when something is measured it will improve, and people are likely to trust evidence from fellow consumers when making choices (Figure 8.1). Ultimately, what is measured should be driven by what is most likely to create a shared culture of improvement within the organization. This is what creates valuable, long-term relationships with customers and enables sustainable growth.

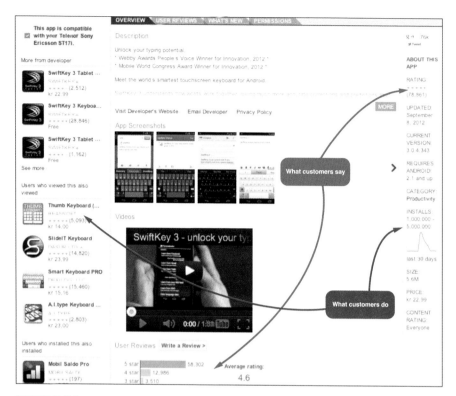

FIGURE 8.1

The Android Market interface includes several examples of how measurement has become an integrated part of the purchasing experience, providing live data both to the provider and to customers.

Establishing a Truth with Management

Top management buy-in is vital to any design effort, and the same goes for measurement. If leaders do not see the strategic reasoning behind measuring something, they are not likely to take the results seriously and act on them. This is particularly true of service design projects because the process often involves a change in cultural mindset within an organization.

One would expect CEOs to base their goals on hard numbers, but when it comes to championing customer experience, committed managers act as much on their own reasoning as on the output of their spreadsheets.

Therefore, designers need to help managers come to their own strong conclusions about what will make their services succeed. Designers can often be very vocal about stepping into the shoes of others when it comes to the end user, but their empathy evaporates when dealing with their clients. CEOs are people, too, with their own needs, motivations, and behaviors, and designers can help them by uncovering and communicating self-evident truths that are simple for CEOs to share with their organizations. Some examples of this are:

- "We are the leader in our sector and can only grow by increasing our margins. Therefore we need to offer the best customer experience."

- "We are a new entry in the market, and need to give customers more for less. Therefore we need to offer the best customer experience."

- "The market is saturated and we need to focus on retaining customers, not acquiring new ones. Therefore we need to offer the best customer experience."

- "Our success depends on acquiring critical mass quickly. Therefore we need to offer the best customer experience."

- "Developing new features is expensive and doesn't provide us with significant competitive advantage. Therefore we need to offer the best customer experience."

- "Customers don't understand how incredibly smart our technology is. Therefore we need to offer the best customer experience."

- "The patients' experience is as important to their well-being as the clinical outcome. Therefore we need to offer the best patient experience."

- "As a monopolist in our market, our customers love to hate us. Therefore we need to offer the best customer experience."

- "The reputation of our products suffers from our neglected customer service. Therefore we need to offer the best customer experience."

This list can go on and applies not only to customer-provider relationships, of course, but also to public service organizations. The point is that managers need simple and logical reasons for investing in service design, which means designers need to support those decisions by measurement.

The most straightforward approach is to establish as a truth that the service experience is crucial to success and then measure how it improves. If the logic is right, the bottom-line numbers will work themselves out when the customer experience improves.

by Lucy Kimbell

When I describe service design to MBAs, they tell me it's what managers already do. Trying to understand customers' lives and needs and then designing offerings that work for them? Check. Using these insights to guide what offerings are created? Check. Aligning organizational resources to deliver particular offerings to particular market segments? Check. Using learning from service interactions to keep an organization focused on continuous improvement? Check.

This response goes to the heart of the issue facing the professionals who specialize in designing services. What service design is about is surely the bread and butter of all organizations. It's what they should be doing, or think they already are doing. Designing services sounds like a mix of marketing, operations management, IT, facilities management, organization design, and human resources, with a bit of change management thrown in.

On closer inspection it looks more like design stuff than management stuff, true. But it is more closely related to the basics of organizations than any other design field. Service design is about people, technology and stuff, processes, and the intersection of all these in the day-to-day operations of any organization in the service of value creation, as defined by its employees, stakeholders, customers, users, regulators, partners, and competitors.

The "what" of service design may seem like the job of managers, not designers. But the "how" is different. And further, the approaches, methods, and skills required to do it (the "how") in fact turn the "what" into something different. The work that managers see as analytical and abstracted becomes generative and materialized. The disconnected stuff of organizational life becomes connected and a shared matter of concern. Organizations are revealed as dynamically constituted in the multiple interactions between people and things and other people, in many places, over time.

The practice of service design (in the version I teach and research) has three key characteristics that make it important to any organizations that have people and purposes to serve, whether they think of themselves as offering services or not. First, service design is centered on an attentiveness to experiences and interactions with digital and material stuff across time and locations. Users are seen as actively involved in creating these experiences, rather than being passive recipients of organizational designs. For users, these interactions constitute the organization, rather than being ancillary to it. So the designing of particular pathways and modes of engagement is central to the work of management, accompanied by an understanding that no encounter can be fully scripted or designed.

Second, it proceeds by creating and using artifacts such as user journeys and blueprints. These are important "boundary objects"[4] that help cross-functional and cross-organizational teams conceptualize and explore from within their specialisms, their shared matter of concern: an

---

4   The term "boundary objects" comes from sociologists studying science; see S. L. Star and J. R. Griesemer, "Institutional Ecology, 'Translations' and Boundary Objects: Amateurs and Professionals in Berkeley's Museum of Vertebrate Zoology, 1907–39," *Social Studies of Science* 19 (1989): 387–420.

organization's services as constituted in the interactions between all sorts of people and stuff. A document such as a blueprint allows different teams to do the work they need to do to create and run a service, and helps them understand how this work relates to that of others, including that of end users. Creating and using such organizational artifacts should be a central concern for managers and project leads, requiring customization of these methods to suit particular organizational contexts and purposes.

Third, the practice of service design involves repeatedly zooming in and out between material and digital detail, and the big picture. Grand narratives or visions describing a service experience or value proposition are necessary. But so, too, are repeated attempts to describe the granular details—the layout of a consulting room, the navigation of a website, or the information design of a ticket. A service design approach requires moving to and fro between each of these, rather than leaving mundane detail until later in a development process, as if it's not so important.

Once exposed to these concepts, the MBA students taking my class find themselves talking and thinking differently about their work. They have a new way of doing what they think is core to their work. And it changes what they think their work is. It sets them on a journey of nurturing and sustaining a designerly culture with their teams in which the practices of experience-based design are embedded.

The approach to designing services described in this book also has implications for design professionals. As discussed here, designing for service reveals itself as more than just a new variant of design. It puts designerly practices at the center of the organizational activity of designing for service. Designers' knowledge and skills make them the right participants to create many of the boundary objects that help teams work together to design services. It gives design professionals opportunities to generate novel methods to articulate and explore service experiences over time and place, and the operational activities that resource these.

It also pushes designers in directions some may not feel comfortable with. It asks them to consider more actively the relationships between the different kinds of digital and material artifacts they design, and their relationships to the backstage operations of organizations or to communities of contributors involved in a networked organizational model. Designers must engage more deeply with understanding and describing different kinds of resources and how these are configured for value creation.

So service design is at once familiar and yet novel. It is what managers and entrepreneurs do already, and yet it makes their work different. It resembles what some designers already do, but asks many others to change. In another decade it might no longer be called service design, but for now it represents a valuable addition to the resources available to anyone designing services.

Lucy Kimbell is associate fellow at Saïd Business School, University of Oxford, where she has been teaching service design to MBA students since 2005.

Apples and Oranges—Define Baseline Data before Design and Launch

To focus the work and make everyone involved more accountable, define what you want to measure when you start the design work. Goals may change along the way as innovative solutions emerge, strategies change, or the competition develops in unexpected ways, but when you approach launch it is essential to establish baseline data to measure against. You need the *before* numbers to prove the success of *after*.

As most designers have experienced, it is difficult to get the numbers that prove pure commercial results from the design input, unless you work in packaging design. Too many factors influence the outcome to attribute it to design alone, but nothing beats cash as evidence of success. Your chances of producing hard economic facts about the effects of the design work will be much higher if you define what you will measure at the start of a project.

Making the Case for Return on Investment

Service providers often struggle to understand the potential return on investment for service design. The key to making the business case for service design is to focus on how you want the work to change customer behavior, and then estimate the potential impact on the business in numbers.

One example of this approach is a process for proving the business value of improved customer experience published by Forrester Research.[5] This model includes the costs and potential benefits of improvements in particular industry sectors, based on changed behavior.

Some typical behaviors often addressed in service design projects can be translated to results on the bottom line:

- New sales: increased acquisition of new customers

- Longer use: increased loyalty and retention of customers

- More use: increase in revenue for every customer

- More sales: increased sales of other services from the same provider

- More self-service: reduced costs

---

5 Megan Burns, with Harley Manning and Jennifer Peterson, "Model the ROI of Customer Experience Improvement Projects: A How-To Guide," Forrester Research report, August 12, 2011, www.forrester.com/rb/Research/ model_roi_of_customer_experience_improvement_projects/q/id/59070/t/2.

- Better delivery processes: reduced costs

- Better quality: increased value for money and competitiveness

When planning a service design project, a smart strategy is to establish key goals right away and assign concrete targets to these, be they commercial, social, or environmental. This will help get managers on board, justify the investment, and provide direction for the design work itself. It also means you will be measured against what you intend to influence, not what someone else decided they could or should measure. You need to make sure you are comparing apples to apples.

When you have determined which behaviors and experiences you want to measure, you need to establish how you can track these to get results that help everyone continue to learn and improve.

Although the list above includes the word "customer," this measurement strategy is as true for nonprofit and public-service projects as it is for commercial ventures. In fact, making the case for investment in design applies even more when public money is involved, especially in times of austerity. As designers, we should be using our empathetic skills to understand what our clients' needs and motivations are, just as much as those of our end users.

Using the Service Blueprint to Model Measurement

What are truly service-native ways to model and measure the value of design? A useful way to approach measurement of services is to return to the service blueprint. The service blueprint has already been used to capture important moments of user interaction with the service, so you already know what you are trying to influence with your design and thus what you want to measure. Therefore, you can use the blueprint not only to plan and design a service, but also as an operational tool to analyze where costs and revenue occur and how they affect the service experience as a whole. The service blueprint can tie together the hard business metrics with the "soft" experience aspects of a service and can ensure that everyone—management, staff, and the design team—is on the same page. You will see below that we look for metrics to measure across time and touchpoint channels just as we did when thinking about the design of the service experience and proposition.

Money Talks

Regardless of our view on design's value to people's lives and experiences, to argue for service design as a business-critical activity, we need simple and useful models that show how revenue flows in a system and how this is directly influenced by design decisions.

Two defining characteristics of service delivery provide a framework for integrating business modeling with the design processes:

1. Services must adapt to people's changing needs over time.

2. People interact with services across multiple touchpoints.

Transformed to points of cost and revenue, these characteristics provide us with a truly service-native way to model a business case and measure the results:

1. Cost and revenue through the customer journey: By breaking down the business model across stages of a customer journey, it is possible to model where costs can be reduced and revenues can be generated in relation to where value is created for the customer.

2. Cost and revenue across touchpoints: By breaking down the business model across touchpoints, it is possible to model in which channels costs can be reduced and revenues can be made while creating value for the customer.

Using the service blueprint to zoom in to the economics of a single interaction with the customer or out to the big picture of the aggregate economics of the service enables managers to prioritize which interactions to invest in, and to analyze whether the whole service proposition will provide a return on investment (Figure 8.2).

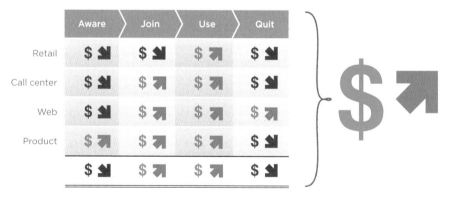

FIGURE 8.2
The service blueprint transformed into business case. Instead of describing design detail, we use the same framework to calculate costs and revenue through the whole customer journey. This tool helps to make the case for investment in creating a great experience in an interaction when the revenue may be regained in another channel or at a later stage.

Avoiding Common Mistakes
When Measuring Services

Measure Experiences over Time

The first mistake organizations typically make when measuring the service experience is to speak with customers or users only once. However, measuring people's experience at different stages of their journey is crucial. Their understanding and expectations will be hugely different when they are new to a service compared to when they have used it for a while.

For example, when people are first admitted to a hospital with a cancer diagnosis, they lack the competence to understand why doctors suggest one treatment over another. Patients need simple facts to cope, and their questions are along the lines of "What are my chances of survival?" After three months of chemotherapy, however, patients may have enough competence to verify that nurses are administering the right dosage, and they can understand enough medical terminology to read the same journal articles as their physicians.

What needs to be measured is whether a service meets people's expectations at different stages. If people have a great experience when they are first sold the service, does it live up to expectations in everyday use? Does a service that is simple to start with give people a greater depth of experience when they gain competency in using it? When do people consider changing providers? How difficult is it for them to leave a service?

To figure this out, you can stay with individual customers and measure their experience over time, or you can engage with several customers at different stages to understand how their expectations and fulfilment change. Most companies want to be great at both acquiring and retaining customers. Measuring along different stages of the customer journey will enable them to do both better. Increased revenue and higher margins should follow naturally.

Measure across Touchpoints

The second common mistake organizations make is to speak with customers who have used only a single service channel. This is fine if you need to understand the quality of a single touchpoint ("What do you think about our website?"), but it will not give you any valuable data about the quality of the service experience as a whole.

Therefore, you need to measure people's experience as they move between touchpoints because this reveals the relationship between expectations and experiences ("Your website was great, but when I tried to speak to a real person I was seriously disappointed. I'm switching to another bank.").

The key thing to learn from measuring across touchpoints is to understand which channels set customer expectations too high to fulfil in the next interaction, and which perform too badly to keep up with the rest of the experience. It is these outliers that destroy the service experience, not the touchpoints that perform to expectation every time.

Share Customer Satisfaction Measurements with Staff

Most corporate employees are used to being measured on key performance indicators that form part of their appraisals and salary negotiations. Usually these are geared to help managers have conversations with staff about productivity and efficiency. Another common mistake, however, is to stick to this top-down view of measurement.

Sharing customer satisfaction data with staff on an ongoing basis can be valuable. Some organizations measure satisfaction after every interaction customers have with staff and report these data back to the individual staff members. Employees can see how well they are measuring up to customers' expectations. Colleagues can compare their performance with others in their units, and can see how their unit performs compared with others.

At first, this may seem like a risky proposition, but it turns out that this feedback is inspiring to staff. It gives them tools to focus on beyond productivity, and lets them engage with the quality that they deliver. It helps staff to highlight system problems that prevent them from providing good service, and provides a sound basis for conversations with colleagues about improving the customer experience.

Ultimately, good customer service is what frontline staff really care about. Most of them are in their positions because they enjoy speaking with people and helping them get things done with a smile on their faces. When you measure service experiences, it pays off if you make the data as transparent as possible to everyone involved and format it to enable collaboration that fosters continual improvement.

Research shows that customer satisfaction scores have a direct relation to a customer's propensity to buy a service and to remain loyal to a provider.

Measurement Frameworks

Net Promoter Score

Within a broad field of methods for measuring satisfaction, one popular framework is the net promoter score. The simplicity of the method is its great advantage—customers are simply asked "How likely is it that you would recommend our company to a friend or colleague?" This type of survey is relatively simple to conduct, and it is constant across companies and industries. This makes it easy for companies to compare their performance with the competition, and good net promoter scores have been documented to relate directly to business growth.

This makes the net promoter score useful in terms of measuring the impact of a new service design. The disadvantage with the method is that it does not tell you much about what you need to do to get better.

The Expectation Gap

More elaborate methods for measuring customer satisfaction dig deeper into how services meet or exceed the expectations people have of them. When you ask customers how satisfied they are and include the context of the time and place of their activity, you are more likely to identify the points where a new design has really made a difference and where the greatest potential for improvement lies.

The challenge with this method is that it requires a systematic approach to measuring customer satisfaction over time. You need to build measurement into the design of the service.

Where we have seen the greatest impact from measurement is in the organizations that routinely ask their customers how satisfied they are with each interaction with the company. These organizations build their own software that triggers surveys after a service interaction, aggregates data across channels and over time, and feeds it back to managers and staff. They also establish routines for reflecting and acting on the results.

This kind of commitment to customer satisfaction from an organization expands the purpose of measurement beyond proving the worth of design and enables cultures of continual improvement. When clients take this commitment seriously, designing the measurement of a service becomes an integrated part of designing the service itself.

As we described in Chapter 1, Norway's largest general insurer, Gjensidige, had bought into the idea that customer satisfaction would be a key strategic direction for the company. As an organization highly oriented to key performance indicators, they had a need to put numbers to their goals. When they established their internal "Extreme Customer Orientation" program, they also needed to put in place company-wide initiatives that went beyond individual improvement projects.

To make their new strategy concrete, they decided to implement a new measurement system focused on the customer experience. The purpose was twofold: to establish a structure that would enforce their new customer-centric philosophy throughout the organization, and to demonstrate by a symbolic effort that experience measures were as important as financial measures.

Several off-the-shelf systems were available that could gather customer satisfaction data, but Gjensidige decided to build their own. In addition to being a cost-effective choice, it enabled them to integrate the data with their existing financial performance measurement system.

The core idea of the measurement system was to implement "individual customer satisfaction scores," meaning that all customer-facing staff would get direct feedback on every interaction they had with customers.

Since 2010, Gjensidige has measured all sales and service interactions with customers on the phone or at their branch offices. They later included all claims interactions in the system. In this way they can measure satisfaction in the three key types of experience customers have with an insurance company: "I need some insurance," "I need to fix something," or "I had an accident and I need help."

Customers are surveyed with a Web questionnaire immediately after each contact, and the questions are tailored to Gjensidige's philosophy, the touchpoint, and the type of interaction customers have just had. Typical focus areas are whether people experience a "first-time fix" and whether customers think they received good advice. On a scale from 0 to 6, if a customer gives a score of 3 or lower, Gjensidige ask if they can contact the customer again to try to improve the situation.

Of all the initiatives the company made in two years to turn themselves into a more customer-centric service provider, the measurement system is the one project that had the greatest single impact on the customer experience.

What It Means to Staff

Managers initially thought twice about how staff would react to being measured on the satisfaction of their customers. It turned out that staff members embraced the feedback with open arms. Responses from customers now go immediately to the staff member they were in contact with. This enables employees who deal with customers every day to reflect on what worked and what didn't work in every conversation. It also enables them to get back to customers who didn't get the outcomes they were after.

Operational managers analyze the data, pull out lessons that can be shared with the team, and activate a call back for customers who give low scores. Gjensidige now reward employees on the basis of both financial and customer satisfaction scores. Yearly bonuses are partly based on customer satisfaction scores, but only on a team level. The realization is that making customers happy is a team effort.

What It Means to Customers

Gjensidige achieve a surprisingly high response rate on their surveys—25% of customers complete them. This rate shows that the surveys were designed in such a way that people perceive them to be a useful way to help Gjensidige achieve a high level of quality.

Of the 70,000 replies received in 2011, only a handful of customers have voiced concern that their feedback could have negative consequences for the person they spoke to, but for the overwhelming majority it opens up a valuable channel for engagement. They see that by helping their insurance company they also help themselves.

What It Means to Management

Since the measurement system was established, the company has amassed a staggering amount of data on how people experience their services. This opens up new spaces for analysis, particularly as it correlates with financial results (Figure 8.3).

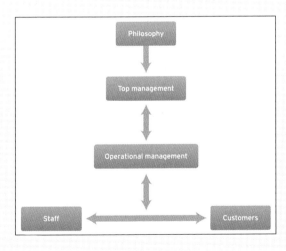

FIGURE 8.3
Customer
satisfaction
data flows
between
customers and
staff as well as
between levels
of management.

sidebar continues on next page

First of all, Gjensidige have seen a significant improvement in customer satisfaction on individual touchpoints over the last two years. From an industry standard of 70% to 80% of customers reporting satisfaction, Gjensidige now deliver scores of more than 85% on the interactions they measure.

Improved touchpoint satisfaction is also reflected in the company's overall customer satisfaction ratings. Customers who have been in contact with the company score higher than those who have not. In other words, the more experiences customers have with Gjensidige, the more they end up as satisfied customers.

In addition, staff who received more training performed better and had more satisfied customers, and a clear correlation was found between customer satisfaction and loyalty. Finally, managers gained evidence that customers who experienced their interaction as "good advice" rather than as "product sales" were more likely to increase their engagement with Gjensidige.

Managers obtained hard numbers to back up their strategy that a focus on customer orientation would produce more profit. This data gave a financial basis for spending money on training and taking on the role of advisor rather than product vendor.

Gaining proof that the strategy worked was a very valuable story for managers—one they could tell their staff, their customers, and their shareholders.

SERVQUAL and RATER

In the 1980s, marketing researchers Valarie Zeithaml, A. Parasuraman, and Leonard Berry developed a service quality framework called SERVQUAL.[6] It was created as a method to manage service quality by measuring gaps between what organizations intend to deliver and what they actually deliver, as well as between people's expectations and their actual experiences with a service.

SERVQUAL can be a great tool both for measuring and designing services, particularly the simplified version commonly known by the acronym RATER, which measures gaps between people's expectations and experience along five key dimensions:

- **Reliability:** the organization's ability to perform the service dependably and accurately

---

6 See Valarie A. Zeithaml, A. Parasuraman, and Leonard L. Berry, "SERVQUAL: A Multiple-Item Scale for Measuring Consumer Perceptions of Service Quality," *Journal of Retailing* 64 (1988): 12–49; or their book *Delivering Quality Service: Balancing Customer Perceptions and Expectations* (New York: Free Press, 1990).

- **Assurance:** employees' knowledge and ability to inspire trust and confidence

- **Tangibles:** appearance of physical facilities, equipment, personnel, and communication materials

- **Empathy:** understanding of customers and acknowledging their needs

- **Responsiveness:** willingness to help customers, provide prompt service, and solve problems

The great thing about RATER for service designers is that these dimensions easily translate into design principles that can be used in projects.

In a call center, for example, *empathy* can be translated into a design principle that states "Always make sure you have understood the customer's problem." The design solution might include in the script for staff a sentence that starts with "Let me check that I understand you correctly . . ." Another solution might be a confirmation e-mail template that starts with "Describe the customer's problem in her/his own words."

Using RATER as a foundation, it is possible to start design projects by defining measurement criteria. From here you can develop design principles and design solutions, and finally, measure the effects of the design. This process completes the loop of measurements and design of a service, but sometimes the consequences of a design reach beyond the service itself and affect society and the environment. This is when you need to apply broader frameworks of measurements, such as the triple bottom line.

The Triple Bottom Line

A useful measurement framework, both to provide design direction and to evaluate results, is the triple bottom line. The concept grew out of the sustainability field and was coined by John Elkington in the late 1990s.[7] The basic concept of the triple bottom line is that an organization should be measured not only by its financial performance, but also by the ecological and social outcomes of what it produces.

The model challenges the idea that companies are responsible to their *shareholders* only, and states that organizations are responsible to their *stakeholders*—anyone who is directly or indirectly affected by the actions of an organization.

The triple bottom line is particularly useful when working with public sector organizations whose ultimate goal is to improve society, but it is increasingly useful in the private sector. The transportation, healthcare, and energy

---

7 John Elkington, *Cannibals with Forks: The Triple Bottom Line of 21st Century Business* (Oxford, UK: Capstone Publishing, 1997).

industries are obvious sectors that have responsibility to communities and to the planet that must be part of the accounting when a new service is designed.

In practice, the triple bottom line is a useful framework when defining the goals of a design project. It helps broaden the scope of the thinking and often challenges clients in a productive way to reflect on the greater ambition of their work.

To return to the Streetcar example, the company's proposition was focused on convenience and economy, but the ecological benefits of car sharing also featured as a selling point for customers. Car sharing also addresses the social need of mobility—it helps people get to work, see friends and family, and go shopping at IKEA (you would be surprised how often this goal comes up in user research about mobility).

When the triple bottom line was used to measure the results of Streetcar after it became a mass-market proposition, the service produced results along all three dimensions (Figure 8.4).

Streetcar ROI: Triple Bottom Line

	Economic	Environmental	Social
Streetcar	Announced profitability within 18 months of launch. Largest club of its kind in the United Kingdom.	Takes an average of 6 privately owned cars off the road per Streetcar. Users drive 69% less.	Expands mobility options of individuals and connectivity between transport modes. Reduces congestion and local pollution.
Customer	A car owner spends on average £4,281.72 per year vs. Streetcar users at £2,523.20 per year. (Royal Automobile Club figure)	63.5% of car club members either give up their cars or don't buy a private vehicle.	Rethinks a behavioral norm (hassle-free mobility). Supports a new social status.

FIGURE 8.4
Streetcar produced results both for the company and for customers: it is a profitable company that saves money for customers, takes cars off the road and greenhouse gases out of the air, and makes it easier for people to combine the use of cars and public transportation.

It is also important to mention that it is not always necessary to account for results purely in terms of numbers. When describing environmental and social effects, sometimes the value to people and the planet are better described in words. It can take a lot of unnecessary work to put a number on the value people derive when a service makes it easier for them to get around, but it can be strongly argued that such a service improves their quality of life, especially when you tell their stories.

Summary

- Service designers and service providers both have a need to prove that design provides a return on investment. It is important to gather your "before" data before you launch in order to be able to contrast this information with the after-launch data to see which design activities have worked or not.

- The metrics should relate to the touchpoint experiences you are trying to improve rather than arbitrary top-down metrics; otherwise, you are not comparing apples to apples. The service blueprint can provide you with a framework that can define what touchpoint interactions should be measured and in what way.

- It is important to measure across the time of the customer journey—not just an individual touchpoint experience in isolation—as well as across channels. Individual touchpoints can score high customer satisfaction ratings, but they also set up expectations for the *transition* to another touchpoint. These transitions are important to take into account because they make up a large part of the service experience.

- Measurement data can be shared with staff as a performance indicator, which aligns the customers' interests with those of the staff. It also provides motivation for an organization's employees.

- Measurement can (and should) take into account the triple bottom line of economic, environmental, and social impacts.

CHAPTER 9

The Challenges Facing Service Design

The issues raised in the measurement of the triple bottom line touch upon the large, complicated problems that affect everyone. In a globalized world, people are dealing with financial, environmental, and social problems on a scale and a level of complexity never before experienced.

Technological shifts may be pushing designers to think about services, but these larger economic, environmental, and social trends are also pulling us toward challenges that are new to design. Change offers a new set of opportunities for designers to expand our remit, break out of the studio, and engage with meaningful work. Creating economically successful organizations through attention to customer and user experience *as well as* addressing the social and ecological challenges outlined in this chapter is the foundation that service designers need to build over the next decade.

In this chapter we look at these three challenging and intertwining areas and how designers can approach them as opportunities to work with businesses, communities, and government agencies to redesign their "operating systems."

Economic Challenges—Moving Businesses from Products to Services

Measurement is critical to showing how our designs impact the classic service goals of customer retention, loyalty, and advocacy to enable organizations to invest more confidently in service design and in new service innovations. But it is also important to amplify the capability of service design by leveraging its ability to connect the economic to the social and ecological in order to make the case for long-term, sustainable (in every sense of the word) change.

Service design has a role to play in shifting economies away from valuing things to valuing benefits, because what is required for this shift is behavior change in two key audiences: organizations need to shift their offers, economics, and operations to orientate around providing access and convenience rather than products alone; and customers need to shift their purchasing decisions from ownership to access and convenience. For both, this means leaving behind a model that they know, trust, and rely on, and accepting something new and less familiar. This is a major challenge that requires vision and motivation.

Design has the capability to provide that vision and to motivate change by providing *desirable* alternatives to trusted norms. Service design is particularly well placed because it connects the business thinking of the service proposition with the actual creation of tangible touchpoints that people will use.

Hilti

A great example of what a shift to service looks like for a product business is construction tool manufacturer Hilti.[1] Hilti makes power tools that it traditionally sold to foremen or construction managers who would own and maintain the tools on behalf of their companies and be responsible for making them available on projects as needed. This responsibility of ownership, logistics, and asset optimization was a burden to the construction companies and their employees. Hilti saw an opportunity to remove these irritations. As the manufacturer, they thoroughly understood the products and had the flexibility of a much larger inventory, so they were in a better position to manage the tool set assets.

Hilti conceived of a service model that offered their customers the tools they needed, where and when they needed them, properly maintained and quickly replaced if they failed. This seems like an obvious step to take, but it required Hilti to develop a whole new way of doing business. Instead of selling tools to foremen on job sites, they now had to sell service contracts to finance directors and then run a service business delivering tools to customers on demand. This required vision and motivation—in this case, motivation from both Hilti and their customers.

Service design is relevant here in two ways. First, we can create these visions through design approaches that understand customer needs and irritations and translate them into opportunities that we can visualize to make them tangible and desirable. Second, we can prototype and run pilots of these new concepts to prove that the service is desirable to customers by staging the service in ways that are real but do not require immediate wholesale change. We can mitigate the risk of change and also create motivation through designed experiences.

From an ecological perspective, Hilti can now do more with less use of natural resources because the service model reduces waste in the system by making material goods work harder for longer, with less downtime and fewer failures. Most important, Hilti are now incentivized to make their tools last as long as possible to gain maximum value from them throughout their life cycle rather than purely at the point of sale. The ecological benefits dovetail into the economic benefits—Hilti can make more money by manufacturing fewer tools, and Hilti's customers have better access to tools while saving money on wasted ownership of tools they don't need.

---

1   Mark W. Johnson, Clayton M. Christensen, and Henning Kagermann, "Reinventing Your Business Model," *Harvard Business Review*, December 2008, www.hbr.org/2008/12/reinventing-your-business-model/ar/1.

Ecological Challenges—
Service Design and Resources

Since the *Limits to Growth* report was issued from the Club of Rome in 1972, awareness has been growing of the finite nature of global natural resources and the limit to the planet's capacity to absorb man-made waste.[2] The most well known and understood of these issues is climate change, with scientific consensus that greenhouse gas emissions are on track to cause significant changes to Earth's climate and will impact humanity in the form of drought, floods, and crop failure. Our demand for finite natural resources is outstripping the speed with which they can be replenished, and their extraction is damaging ecosystems. We are all aware of the impact of deforestation on other species, but it also impacts humanity in places like Bangladesh and Pakistan, where cleared land no longer absorbs rainfall, leading to extreme flooding of low-lying villages, towns, and cities.

A complete catalogue of ecological challenges is beyond the scope of this book; however, we do want to explore the role design, and specifically service design, has in addressing these challenges.

Underlying most ecological issues is the industrial mode of operation and thinking. The industrial revolutions and resulting material wealth have been powered by fossil fuels—from coal to gas to oil—and have relied on readily available natural resources to feed human consumer societies. Notions of wealth and value are built on physical things—the wealth of nations is measured in terms of gross domestic *product*. Major corporations depend, in the main, on constantly selling more products. Consider the automotive industry as an example. In 2011 the number of cars in the world surpassed 1 billion, and yet the primary goal of auto manufacturers is to sell more cars. To do this they must open up new markets, which is clearly unsustainable, and yet it is the dominant economic model of success based on continuous, infinite growth on a planet that has finite resources.

The chink of light in this situation are the growing service economies and the trends in consumer demand away from ownership toward a better understanding of value and utility. Service design has a role to play in speeding the shift to a more resource-efficient economic model that uses service as a means to decouple value from resources. As individuals, we begin to look for the best form of mobility rather than desire to own a car; we sign up to subscription services, such as Netflix, rather than hoarding stacks of DVDs that we will never watch more than twice; and we share tools with our neighbors through services like Neighborgoods.net instead of leaving them idle in our toolbox

---

2   Donella H. Meadows, Dennis L. Meadows, Jørgen Randers, and William W. Behrens III, *The Limits to Growth* (New York: Universe Books, 1972). The Club of Rome has published a "30-Year Update" of the book; see http://cluberome.at/archive/limits.html.

(the average drill is used a total of 12 to 13 minutes during its lifetime). What we actually need is the experience or utility—to get from point A to point B, to watch a film, or to make a hole in the wall—not the product.

In these kinds of collaborative consumption and redistribution models, the personal value is in the convenience and access rather than burden of ownership, but the aggregate value is ecological (and, quite often social, because such services can help reconnect people within neighborhoods).[3]

For a service to replace a product, it must be tangible, useful, and desirable, and service design provides an approach to designing these services. Many solutions to ecological issues ask people to stop doing something without offering an alternative, but it is much easier to offer people an alternative than it is to ask them to give up something.

It is not that products disappear completely—most services are product-service systems that combine service and product elements—but the opportunity is to do more with less. An organization providing products as part of a service can make more money from a single car, DVD, or drill because that object is providing more value to more people. The service adds value over and above that of the original manufacturer of the product. Services that use networks to connect people act as multipliers to these individual shifts in resource usage and can reflect the effect of those multiplied changes back to people in ways that inspire further shifts in behavior.

Hafslund

One example of a design change aimed at effecting behavioral change is the invoice redesign for Norway's largest utilities provider, Hafslund. A lot of calls were being fielded in Hafslund's call center from customers who did not understand their bills. The primary goal of the design work was to make the bill easier to understand, which would improve customer experience and loyalty and reduce call center traffic.

It was also an opportunity to use the invoice to nudge people toward reducing their energy consumption. A color-coded box added to the bill clearly indicated whether customers were using more or less energy than during the same period the year before. By incorporating the feature in the new invoice, Hafslund showed customers that they offered more of a service than just providing electricity through the wall socket and that they were concerned with more than just profits. Helping to develop collective responsibility for the environment is also part of their service (Figure 9.1).

---

3 For an excellent resource of examples, see www.collaborativeconsumption.com/
the-movement/snapshot-of-examples.php, the companion website for Rachel Botsman
and Roo Rogers, *What's Mine Is Yours: The Rise of Collaborative Consumption* (New York:
HarperBusiness, 2010).

FIGURE 9.1
The green box states, "Your electricity consumption in March and April this year is 13% lower than in the same period last year. Call this free number to get advice on how you can save energy." The orange box indicates an increase in energy consumption.

In this case, triple bottom line thinking helped introduce new features that customers appreciated. Hafslund's bill redesign saved them money because it reduced the number of calls to the call center, but the company's choice to add value by providing customers with information to help them save energy has impacted the environment in a positive way. In the future, the aim is to measure whether Hafslund's customers stay loyal to them and whether they are willing to pay a premium price for taking collective responsibility for the environment.

Social Challenges— Service Design for Improving Society

From the outset, our ambition as service designers was to work with public services. Initially, this was because we felt we should not ignore such a large segment of the market. As we have learned more about public services, we have teamed up with a number of other designers and design advocates who see a role for service design in addressing key issues that public services face. Although service designers are new to this space compared with the policy makers, social scientists, and economists who dominate public debate, it is precisely because we are not public service natives that we bring something different and valuable to the table as people try to rethink and change public services.

In the public services sphere, such as education, welfare, and healthcare, the legacy of industrial thinking shows just how far the production-line model has spread. The same industrial thinking that we have challenged as inadequate to the nature of services is also proving inadequate to address today's social challenges.

There is growing recognition in developed countries that public services and the welfare state were established in a different time for different needs and that major social challenges, such as aging populations and the prevalence of chronic disease, mean that we will have to dramatically rethink these services. The very real concern is that services will become unaffordable and that they are not meeting the needs of the people they are meant to help. In the United Kingdom, public service innovation group Participle (www.participle.net) argues that the welfare state is in need of radical rethinking to meet the challenges of the 21st century.

For example, two pillars of public service in the United Kingdom are the National Health Service and the comprehensive school system. Both are fantastic efforts to bring healthcare and education to everyone. They address two of the "great evils"—disease and ignorance (the others being want, squalor, and idleness)—as defined by British social reformer William Beveridge in 1942. [4] We now take for granted many of the achievements of these reforms in the same way that we take industrial products for granted—they, like the washing machine, have raised our standard of living and deserve our gratitude.

Yet, these monumental projects have an industrial mode of operation—the mass production of literacy or disease eradication. Hospitals and schools can seem like factories, and people's experiences of these institutions can be impersonal. More important, these institutions may be reaching the limits of their capacity to deal with the issues they were created to resolve.

Taking the example of healthcare, we can see that although people no longer live in fear of many of the diseases that were still deadly in the 1940s, they are now faced with a number of chronic conditions (such as diabetes and hypertension) that are severely debilitating and cost a fortune to deal with. These already account for 75% of US healthcare costs. [5] In simple terms, large high-tech hospitals are not the solution for these woes.

---

4 For those readers not familiar with William Beveridge, see Wikipedia's entry about him: http://en.wikipedia.org/wiki/William_Beveridge.

5 Centers for Disease Control and Prevention, "Chronic Disease Prevention and Health Promotion," www.cdc.gov/chronicdisease/overview/index.htm; and Chronic Disease Indicators database, http://apps.nccd.cdc.gov/cdi/.

In the case of education, we have found through our own work with young people and employment services that, although schools are providing literacy for most students, some young people are not connecting with the school system and feel that they have wasted their time at school. They leave with few prospects and, in the worst cases, their confidence has been ruined by their inability to achieve in school. These young people need something from the school system that it is not capable of delivering.

In both of these cases the industrial model dominates. To be a patient in a hospital is to move from one processing station to another, like some kind of healthcare assembly line. The dominant management concept in hospitals is one of increasing efficiency and cost savings (particularly in the United Kingdom at the time of this writing). Patient healthcare is second in priority, despite government rhetoric, and the experience of patients receiving or medical staff providing that healthcare is trailing along in the distance.

Educational institutions suffer a similar problem. It is no coincidence that the spread of mass public education coincided with the Industrial Revolution. Families moved from rural areas to cities to work in factories. Children needed to be cared for while their parents worked, and they needed to be educated (although some children ended up working in factories, too). The style of this mass education matched the jobs the children were likely to get in the factories, requiring them to sit still, be quiet, do what they were told, and learn tasks by rote and routine. If you compare a classroom and its rows of desks with a sweatshop and its rows of sewing machines, the resemblance is not a coincidence.

Efficiency and cost savings are at odds with providing a positive educational experience for students. The metrics being used to measure success are usually only those that are easy to measure in numbers, which tends to be grade average in subjects that are suited to this kind of grading. As everyone knows, the school experience adds up to much more than this. Many subjects are about making connections and having discussions and experiences. Most people's grades on their school exams fade into irrelevance over the years, but the shared experiences or wise, touching words from a teacher can stay with people for a lifetime. But because it is hard to pin a number on these experiences, they stay out of the metrics.

In higher education the industrial model is largely the same. New students are raw material that must be stamped into the shape of a particular profession. Accountants, doctors, lawyers, designers, and social workers all roll off the end of the production line with degrees—and debt—in hand.[6]

---

6   Sir Ken Robinson has written and spoken extensively about this topic
    (see http://sirkenrobinson.com/skr/) as has Seth Godin (see www.squidoo.com/
    stop-stealing-dreams).

It is clear by now that politicians and policy makers are struggling to tackle the big challenges and changes described in this chapter, but it is important to emphasize that we are not saying that service designers are going to take over and solve everything as some kind of design superheroes. The issues that service design uncovers and the solutions that it offers involve significant change management on organizational as well as political and cultural levels, and it is important that we work with professionals in those areas, as well as policy makers and advisors, to make sure the change actually happens. These kinds of partnerships only work when there is a climate of professional humility on all sides.

A good example is the UK-based social innovation organization The Young Foundation (www.youngfoundation.org). The foundation's team comprises researchers, ethnographers, policy experts, general practitioners, and former management consultants. The foundation has been using service design approaches to design a new social enterprise, Care 4 Care (http://care4care.org), which uses time-banking principles to support people in creating additional care capacity and enable older people to live better lives and stay longer in their homes.

The foundation has also worked with affordable housing provider Metropolitan (www.metropolitan.org.uk) to help design a befriending service, again to reach older people in their homes, and also with staff and users of the hostels run by People Can (www.peoplecan.org.uk) to help bring the experiences of service users into the design of the organization's housing and support services around the United Kingdom.

Make It Work

Although the service design model of measuring across time and touch-points is actually quite simple, it has proven to be useful in complex cases. One of these is a project to reduce unemployment carried out with the City of Sunderland in northeast England. The city found itself in a particularly challenging situation in which, out of 37,000 unemployed residents, only 5,000 were actively seeking employment. The journey from worklessness back to work needed to be redesigned.

In public service design and innovation, success cannot be measured by competitive advantage, but rather by the value it brings to society. This is hard to measure, particularly in the multifaceted network of a community. With Sunderland, however, we were able to first present a credible business case for investing in a service pilot and later measure the results of the pilot to argue for a large-scale deployment of new services.

Sunderland has suffered more than most from the decline of heavy industry in England. Affected by the loss of both the coal mining and shipbuilding industries, the city has some of the highest rates of unemployment in the United Kingdom. Many people have never worked and come from families who have not known reliable employment for generations.

This setting provided the context for our work with the City Council on the project in 2005, which was supported by One NE, the regional development agency. The brief was to redesign the journey to work for long-term unemployed people, especially those with complex reasons for their unemployment, such as bad health, substance addiction, or caring responsibilities. It was necessary to look at the whole journey and, specifically, to develop a solution that was primarily informed by end user needs.

Starting with Fieldwork

The research involved in-depth fieldwork with a small number of individuals within a specific area of Sunderland. Researchers from the service design team shadowed participants' days to understand how they lived, focusing on the interactions they had with services such as healthcare, social services, employment offices, and voluntary groups. From this work it was possible to construct an ideal but realistic blueprint of what needed to be in place for these people to make their journey back to work. The journey is based on overcoming barriers and is informed by the insight that people are not able to think about work until their more pressing needs, such as health and housing, are under control.

The blueprint, based on user needs, was then used as a common structure for all the partners on the project to organize themselves around. Health teams were able to see how they contributed to employment by getting people well, while rehab programs could connect to employment resources to help their clients' progress. All the services came together to support individuals in becoming self-sufficient.

The blueprint made clear improvements in the user experience of employment support services. It also helped managers focus their resources on where they were most effective. However, it was also necessary to demonstrate that the activity was cost effective overall and for each specific activity. We needed to show that the idea the blueprint modeled was financially viable.

The Case for Investment

The business case for investment was based on the blueprint designed during this first phase of the project (Figure 9.2).

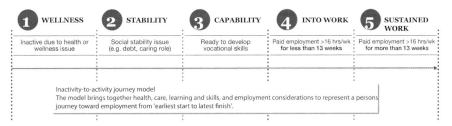

FIGURE 9.2

The five stages of getting back to employment provided the timeline for the Make It Work blueprint.

There is not a specific number for how much one unemployed person costs society, but we were able to find that the state spends between £10,000 and £40,000 per person out of work, per year, in benefits and other social costs. We knew the rates of worklessness in Sunderland, the services being offered along the customer journey, and what it would cost to redesign these services. We now had a metric for calculating the value of our design intervention.

We calculated that a reasonable goal would be that for every £1 invested, there would be a £2 savings to the public purse—a 100% return on investment. If scaled up, the benefits would be massive—100 people in work would create a minimum £1 million in savings per year. Remember, the city had 37,000 people out of work.

The City Council believed in the potential defined by this initial project, and the insights and concepts were shared in workshops with more than 200 operational council employees to enable them to improve their services.

Making It Work

The blueprint made sense on paper and the service activity was aligned to a cost-benefit model, but it was important to demonstrate that it worked in practice. To do this, we needed to understand how all the different departments and organizations would work together, so we needed to go beyond small experience prototypes and design a pilot project that would apply the principles on a small scale but involve as many of the partners as possible (Figure 9.3). This way we could test the activities before taking the service to the whole city.

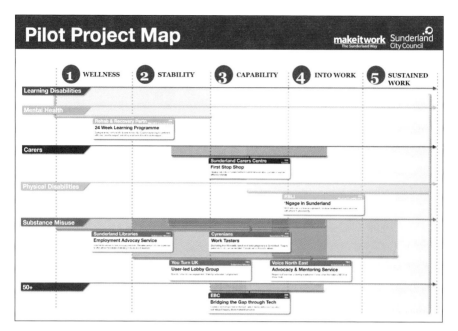

FIGURE 9.3

The pilot project map shows how a series of services were structured along the customer journey to provide different client groups with tailored offerings in a progression toward sustained work.

For the pilot, a number of complementary services—both from the public and voluntary sectors—were commissioned to work together to test the blueprint. All parties would use the journey to work as their model and collaborate to ensure that their clients had their needs met in the order outlined in the blueprint.

During the pilot, the knowledge that it takes time to help people into work became tangible. It became evident that, although some people would make it into work, others would only begin their journey, perhaps overcoming a major barrier but not finding a job. It was clear that there was value in this activity in the long term and also immediately within the funding term of the pilot, but this value needed to be demonstrated to the project sponsor. To do this, the costs and benefits were aligned with the service blueprint. It was then possible to uncover the savings to society of eliminating homelessness or addiction and apply them to individual cases. We also knew the cost per person of all of the partners in the pilot, so we were able to make a cost-benefit calculation for each step of the journey (Figure 9.4).

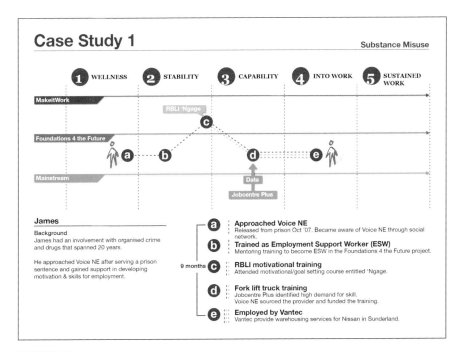

Case Study 1   Substance Misuse

① WELLNESS   **②** STABILITY   **③** CAPABILITY   **④** INTO WORK   **⑤** SUSTAINED WORK

MakeitWork

RBLI 'Ngage
c

Foundations 4 the Future
a ---- **b**   **d** ---- **e**

Mainstream
Data
Jobcentre Plus

James

Background
James had an involvement with organised crime
and drugs that spanned 20 years.

He approached Voice NE after serving a prison
sentence and gained support in developing
motivation & skills for employment.

9 months

a **Approached Voice NE**
Released from prison Oct '07. Became aware of Voice NE through social
network.

b **Trained as Employment Support Worker (ESW)**
Mentoring training to become ESW in the Foundations 4 the Future project.

c **RBLI motivational training**
Attended motivational/goal setting course entitled 'Ngage.

d **Fork lift truck training**
Jobcentre Plus identified high demand for skill.
Voice NE sourced the provider and funded the training.

e **Employed by Vantec**
Vantec provide warehousing services for Nissan in Sunderland.

FIGURE 9.4

In the case of individual clients, we tracked their journey through the system
to see how they engaged with different service offerings on their path toward
work. One of these was James, who after serving a prison sentence went on to
work as a forklift truck driver for Nissan.

The Social and Economic Return on Investment

Over a period of nine months, a range of organizations in Sunderland partnered to pilot a series of service concepts with 238 workless "clients." Of
these, 19 people had come into sustained work during the pilot. Just as
important, 38 people had gone from being unable to work to being capable
of working, and 72 people in total had jobs safeguarded. The results showed
that the redesigned services could bring huge benefits to the community
(Figure 9.5).

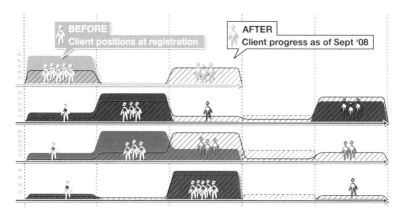

FIGURE 9.5

The Make It Work pilot included people who were out of work for different reasons—from people suffering from mental health or substance abuse problems to people who took care of family members or were over 50 and did not fit into the local labor market. This chart shows how the people in the different groups progressed toward work during the nine months of the pilot.

The Revenue Potential

After completion of the pilot, the data collected was used to estimate the costs and success rate of the design of the new services. To model the revenue potential, we broke down average savings for society per user into five well-documented categories. The model included economic costs such as:

- Estimated benefits costs—what the city no longer had to pay each individual in benefits

- Estimated exchequer losses/gains—the tax people pay when employed

- Economic output losses/gains—the value employed people create for their employers

- Health and social externalities—the value attached to improved health and reduced social problems

Personal cost impacts were also included in the model, even if they were hard to estimate and are not traditionally counted. The personal price of unemployment can range from social exclusion to excess mortality rates.

Savings for Every Step of the Journey

It is easy to assume that return on investment would only happen when people got permanent jobs, but this was not the whole picture. Using the business model, it was possible to demonstrate how Sunderland would be able to save money for every step clients took along the journey back to work, not just once they had reached their final goal of having a job.

For example, a person who manages to overcome mental health problems and progress toward work would save the community £4,000 simply by becoming *capable* of working. Savings would rise up to £20,000 if the same person managed to get into sustained work (Figure 9.6).

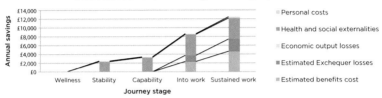

FIGURE 9.6
The rising savings to the city of a person moving through the stages of getting back into sustained employment.

Based on the pilot, we now had data on what the costs of service provision were along the customer journey, as well as for different target groups. We also had data on the success rate of the new service design and its estimated savings, and we could calculate return on investment for a full-scale launch of the new design.

The service pilot showed that for a cost of £180,000, the community had saved £435,000 (Figure 9.7). This gave concrete numbers for estimating a 140% return on investment for a full-scale launch.

Mental Health

	Wellness	Stability	Capability	Into work	Sustained work	Total	Estimated costs		Cost per person	
Opening	39	1	0	0	0	40		£33,750		£844
Closing	18	0	22	0	0	40	Estimated savings		Saving per person	
Net change	-21	-1	22	0	0			£79,335		£1,983

Substance users

	Wellness	Stability	Capability	Into work	Sustained work	Total	Estimated costs		Cost per person	
Opening	5	23	9	0	0	37		£58,750		£1,588
Closing	1	6	22	0	8	37	Estimated savings		Saving per person	
Net change	-4	-17	13	0	8			£102,792		£2,778

Carers

	Wellness	Stability	Capability	Into work	Sustained work	Total	Estimated costs		Cost per person	
Opening	21	65	1	0	50	137		£43,750		£319
Closing	14	55	7	3	58	137	Estimated savings		Saving per person	
Net change	-7	-10	6	3	8			£193,855		£1,415

Over 50s users

	Wellness	Stability	Capability	Into work	Sustained work	Total	Estimated costs		Cost per person	
Opening	4	0	20	0	0	24		£43,750		£1,823
Closing	2	2	17	0	3	24	Estimated savings		Saving per person	
Net change	-2	2	-3	0	3			£58,834		£2,451

Totals

	Wellness	Stability	Capability	Into work	Sustained work	Total	Estimated costs	
Opening	69	89	30	0	50	238		£180,000
Closing	35	63	68	3	69	238	Estimated savings	
Net change	-34	-26	38	3	19			£434,817

FIGURE 9.7
The total cost savings of the Make It Work pilot project.

The Make It Work project demonstrates a highly complex case involving a broad set of stakeholders and a public service context where performance cannot simply be measured in profit. Using the framework of a service blueprint presented the opportunity to model a service-native business case and merge it with the design process. It illustrates the common ground possible for design, economics, and social policy.

Tackling Wicked Problems

Social challenges are wicked problems.[7] These are complex, intertwined with many other problems, and probably not "solvable" in the way we are used to thinking about solving problems. In most developed countries, however, approaches to social challenges have two facets: they aim to address a defined goal, and they need to do it within limited means.

In a democracy, people aim to achieve the best possible level of agreement on these goals and the resources they deserve. For example, a teacher aims to help her class achieve a set level of literacy over the academic year, but must do this with the limited time and attention that she has for each individual in a class of 30 children. Class sizes are a factor of education budgets.

Applying service design to a social context means understanding these twin drivers and understanding the needs of all the stakeholders. Designers need to engage with the public policy world that defines goals in terms of social goods (literacy in our example) and also understand the resource limitations that the service works within.

A major challenge for services in a social context is that the defined goals, although hopefully democratically defined, can easily be disconnected from the goals of all the people involved both in service provision and as service beneficiaries. Service design offers a way to examine the fit between the two and recommend new ways to connect people that achieve goals and also reduce the demands placed on limited resources.

Socially beneficial services have a different relationship dynamic to commercial services. A commercial service that the customer pays for is a relatively straightforward relationship. To make a phone call, the customer pays by the minute for that call. The company's goal is to sell as many calls as possible.

---

7 Jon Kolko's *Wicked Problems: Problems Worth Solving* is a good resource for designing for "wicked problems." It is available to read online for free at www.wickedproblems.com.

We need to understand that in a social context there is no customer. Not the students, the parents, or the teacher. This means that the driver of the service is often the government agency that set the policy goals that may or may not be aligned with the goals of the other people involved. Teachers may have different ideas about what value means in education; parents certainly want different things for their children; and the children themselves want something different from their school day. A service design approach to understanding people and relationships can uncover the disconnects between the goals and motivations of all the different actors.

Socially beneficial services have a wider social value to the health of society as well as being valuable to the individual. Services such as healthcare, education, and welfare insurance benefit the national well-being and economy. Police, prisons, and probation services are also, generally, seen as socially beneficial in terms of public safety, if not directly beneficial to some individuals. The relationships that the service consists of are different. Even if we are the direct customers of the service, the provider organization is not motivated to simply sell us more. They will often, in fact, wish to reduce our usage, or in healthcare parlance "discharge" us from the service.

In the case of some services from which we personally benefit, such as healthcare, we would ideally not be using the service at all; we would rather simply not be ill in the first place, and healthcare providers and insurers are happy if we stay healthy. If the service is prison, we clearly do not want to use it at all and may or may not benefit personally from its use in the long term. Ideally, of course, prison would actually benefit and not just punish those imprisoned there, which in turn would benefit society. Sometimes this happens, but all too rarely.

Where do motivations and interests lie? In some instances, such as healthcare, we may have a huge personal interest in the success of the service (our own life chances). In others, the benefit may be one that we are not personally convinced is in our interest, but may be of benefit to society (taxation is a good example of this). In other services, the benefit can be too distant for the service user to grasp at the time, such as the benefits of education to a young child.

The opportunity for service design is to use insights research to understand the nature of the relationships and identify the motivations of the people involved, to define opportunities for new ways for the different parties to achieve their goals. The service design toolkit contains some invaluable approaches that can be used to rethink public services. These can help designers move from an industrial way of thinking about these issues and help deal with the complexity and multiple stakeholders that are inherent in services.

Service Design for a Better World

In the United Kingdom, companies like Participle (www.participle.net), which work with and for the public to develop new kinds of public services, and organizations like Demos (www.demos.co.uk) and The New Economics Foundation (www.neweconomics.org), think tanks that focus on politics and economics respectively, are working hard to unpick and rethink these complex social problems.

On a global level, service design approaches are being used more and more often in areas such as peace, security, and development within organizations such as The Policy Lab (www.thepolicylab.org) and The United Nations Institute for Disarmament Research (http://unidir.org). These organizations are working at the highest levels of development and security policy, examining life-and-death scenarios in some of the most dangerous countries in the world. There is a recognition that the old "best practice" way of approaching this kind of work no longer suffices, but that a shift toward a "best process," which design can contribute to, is a possible way to rethink international intervention in these countries. At the same time, these peace, security, and development professionals caution designers to be more rigorous about the cases they put forward because the outcomes are at a very different level. A poorly designed website might mean a frustrating purchasing experience, but a poorly designed development or disarmament project might mean the death of many people.

Service design is also being employed in bottom-of-the-pyramid social entrepreneurship projects.[8] Bottom-of-the-pyramid projects target the 5 billion people who live on less than $2.50 per day—those at the bottom of the economic pyramid—but who, collectively, have enormous buying power. These projects are not aid projects, but sustainable business models that deliberately target this extremely low-income demographic to provide them with products and services to improve their lives. The results of these projects are measured in terms of social change as well as business success—both are crucial for sustainable, long-term change.

Companies like Reboot (http://thereboot.org) in New York are using service design methods, combined with traditional development methods, to help rethink governance and international development projects. Service design offers the connection of field research into the lives, needs, and behaviors of people on the ground to the design, development, and implementation of these business and services. It offers a bottom-up perspective and process to policies that have been traditionally implemented from above and afar (some aid agency managers are tasked with sending millions of dollars to countries they have never even visited).

---

8 C. K. Prahalad, *The Fortune at the Bottom of the Pyramid: Eradicating Poverty Through Profits*, rev. 5th ed. (Upper Saddle River, NJ: Wharton School Publishing, 2010).

Service design excels at dealing with complexity, breaking it down into its composite parts while still understanding the whole. Many other disciplines do this in other areas, of course, but services and the exchange of service value are central to our lives and the complex social, ecological, and economic problems we face, and we need a services mindset to tackle them. Crucially, service design provides not only a different way of just thinking about these problems, but the tools and methods to tackle them through design, implementation, and measurement.

The industrial model has served a small percentage of humanity well for the last 150 years, but it has unleashed a host of other problems that we now must face. Clearly, service design is not a panacea. Its future is in collaboration within multidisciplinary teams and with multiple stakeholders, as the examples in this book and from the organizations mentioned above demonstrate. As much as it is important for service designers to have an understanding of the economics and management concerns of business, the complexities of climate change, or the history of international development, it is perhaps more important to learn to work closely with experts in these areas. Service design is a powerful addition to the range of approaches that we need to design a better, more inclusive, and thoughtful future.

Index

N

National Health Service (UK), 177
needs
  services adaptation to, 160
  services providing response to, 30–31
net promoter score, 163
network services, 24
network society, 85–86
New Economics Foundation, 188
Norway. *See also* Gjensidige (Norway)
  employment and public benefits, 5
Norwegian National Customer Satisfaction Barometer, 16
numbers, insights vs., 38–46

O

Occupy Wall Street movement, 81
offer sent in mail, prototype, 14
One NE, 180
opportunities, lost by enterprises, 81
options for services, 5
Orange (mobile operator), 20–21
orchestral metaphors, in service design,
  92–93
organizational charts, 86

P

paper-based routines, 8–9
Parasuraman, A., 166
participant observation, 54–57
participants, in prototype, 144
participation prototypes, 142
Participle, 177, 188
peer education program, 42
peer-to-peer lending service, 110–115
people
  designing *with*, not *for*, 41
  as heart of services, 36–37
  services co-production by, 23–24
  views of banks, 113
People Can, 179
perceived quality, 137
perception, changing for education
  classes, 43

performance indicators, definition in
  proposals, 152
performance measurement, 7
performance of services, 31–33
personal component, in customer
  relations, 7
personalizing services, 38
personal routines, formalizing, 8–9
phase and step summaries, 121–124
phase summary document, 123
photograph lists, 67
photos, interviews and, 70–71
pilot prototyping, 143
The Policy Lab, 188
preparation
  for experience prototypes, 143–146
  for research, 70
presenting insights, 73–76
prioritizing project issues, 49
probes and tools, 62–69
  brand sheets, 65–66
  cameras, 66–67
  diaries, 64–65
  item labels, 68–69
  photograph lists, 67
  preparing, 63
  timelines and journey maps, 63
  Venn diagrams, 65
  visual interpretations, 68
process diagrams, 86
processes, redesigned, 8
product innovation, time delay in, 10
production-line model, 177
production, measuring efficiences in, 152
products
  services vs., 19–22
  transition to services, 103–105
  value of, 113–114
prototype. *See also* experience prototypes
  for contract, 13
  for insurance service, 11–14
public benefits, filling in gaps, 6–7
public services
  development of new types, 188
  human experience in, 136
punctuality, cultural expectations, 70

ACKNOWLEDGMENTS

Thanks to our editor, JoAnn Simony, and to our publisher, Lou Rosenfeld, for their enormous patience, support, and guidance as we hashed out the structure of this book and knocked it into shape. Thanks also to the Rosenfeld production team for all their work getting the book into its print and digital forms.

Thank you to Dave Gray and Jess McMullin, who reviewed the early manuscript, and special thanks to John Thackara, who also reviewed the manuscript and wrote the inspiring Foreword.

Thanks to Chris Risdon, Lucy Kimbell, John Kolko, and Christina Tran for their contributions from their practice, and to all of the staff at live|work, both past and present, whose thoughts, practical tips, and work appear throughout the book. Much of the text on insights research tips and tricks comes from Rory Hamilton and Jaimes Nel sharing their experiences. In particular we wish to thank John Holager and Anders Kjeseth Valdersnes, who helped set up the live|work Oslo office, and Tennyson Pinheiro and Luis Alt, who brought live|work to Brazil. Our thanks also to Gjensidige for allowing us to publish the extensive case study of their business, and to Giles Andrews from Zopa and Joe Gebbia from Airbnb, who both gave their time to talk to us about their innovative business models.

Finally, thanks to all the many people upon whose shoulders we stand and upon whose work service design has been built.

***

Thanks to my family for their support, and to my colleagues, conference attendees, service design community, and Twitter followers for helping me refine my ideas. Thanks are due to my students, whose challenging questions and problems have helped clarify my own. I would also like to acknowledge the memory of Andy Cameron, who passed away in 2012 at far too young an age. He was a mentor for me, and his insight and intellect greatly shaped my own thoughts about people, culture, interactive media, and as a result, service design. Finally, thanks to Ben and Lavrans for being my co-authors. Any errors or omissions in the book are, of course, entirely their fault.

—Andy Polaine

***

First of all, thanks to Chris Downs, the original founder of live|work, for his exceptional creativity, generous intelligence, and insulting sense of humor. The experience of starting live|work together was a gift beyond our dreams.

Thanks to Gillian Crampton Smith, who first introduced us to the history and future of interaction design at the Royal College of Art at the end of the last century, and then helped us develop service design through teaching at the Interaction Design Institute Ivrea at the beginning of the new century.

Thanks to mentor and friend Birgitta Cappelen for never-ending inspiration and support.

Bill Moggridge, who sadly passed away shortly before publication of this book, was a huge inspiration and support for our practice and our writing. We would have loved to show this book to him.

Thanks to Colin Burns for practical support in the early years of live|work.

Thanks to all our engaged and passionate clients and partners with whom we have broken new ground. You are too many to mention, but you know who you are.

Finally, thanks to Andy, who got the idea for this book off the ground, continually drove the writing process forward, and committed to the tremendous task of single-handedly making it all come together in the end. This is your book.

—Lavrans Løvlie and Ben Reason

ABOUT THE AUTHORS

Andy Polaine has been involved in interaction design since the early 1990s and was co-founder of the award-winning new media group Antirom in London. He was a creative producer at Razorfish (UK), and later Interactive Director at Animal Logic in Sydney. Andy was Senior Lecturer and Head of the School of Media Arts at The University of New South Wales, and holds a PhD from the University of Technology, Sydney, in which he examined the relationship between play and interactivity. Now living in Germany, he divides his time between being a Research Lecturer in Service Design at the Lucerne School of Art and Design, Switzerland, and his work as an independent service and interaction design consultant and writer. His personal site is Playpen (www.polaine.com/playpen), and he can be found on Twitter as @apolaine.

***

Lavrans Løvlie has worked as a design consultant since 1994. Before setting up live|work in London with Chris Downs and Ben Reason, he worked as an interaction designer in Norway and Denmark. As a partner in live|work, Lavrans has been the lead designer on service innovation projects for Sony Ericsson, Sony, Samsung, Aviva/Norwich Union, the BBC, Oslo University Hospital, Johnson & Johnson, the United Kingdom's Design Council, Orange, and Vodafone. He has also served on the committee responsible for the British Standard for Service Design.

Lavrans has lectured and run seminars at the Interaction Design Institute Ivrea (Italy), Köln International School of Design (Germany), Oslo School of Architecture (Norway), Institute of Health and Society at the University of Oslo, University of Art and Design Helsinki (Finland), the Estonian Academy of Arts, and Cranfield School of Management (UK). He also serves as a board member at the Norwegian Design Council.

***

Ben Reason is a co-founder of live|work. He graduated from Liverpool John Moores University in 1994 with a BA in Fine Arts, followed in 2000 with an MSc in Responsibility and Business Practice from the University of Bath. Ben has a background in design and innovation in network-enabled services, and prior to live|work worked with Web agencies Razorfish and Oyster Partners.

Ben has provided strategic guidance and project delivery management on a range of high-profile projects for organizations such as the NHS, BBC, UK Home Office, Johnson & Johnson, and Transport for London. In 2009 he was voted one of the top 20 most influential designers in *IKON* magazine. Ben has taught service design at Goldsmiths London, Interaction Design Institute Ivrea, and the Royal College of Art.